ALCATRAZ

THE ULTIMATE
MOVIE BOOK

ROBERT LIEBER

GOLDEN GATE NATIONAL PARKS CONSERVANCY
SAN FRANCISCO, CALIFORNIA

The Golden Gate National Parks Conservancy is a nonprofit membership organization created to help preserve the Golden Gate National Parks, enhance the experiences of park visitors, and build a community dedicated to conserving the parks for the future. For more information about the Parks Conservancy, please call (415) 4R-PARKS, or visit *www.parksconservancy.org*. For park information, please visit *www.nps.gov/alcatraz*.

Library of Congress Control Number: 2005931751
ISBN 1-883869-92-7

DESIGN: Vivian Young, Parks Conservancy
EDITOR: Susan Tasaki, Parks Conservancy
PHOTO RESEARCH AND GENERAL ASSISTANCE: Sarah Lau, Parks Conservancy
NATIONAL PARK SERVICE ADVISORS: Rich Weideman, Ricardo Perez, Craig Glassner, and John Cantwell

Printed on recycled paper in Hong Kong through Global Interprint, Santa Rosa, CA.

Photography Credits

Photographs included in this book are from a number of sources, and may be protected by copyright or have other use restrictions. For use-related questions, please contact the relevant individual or archive.

FRONT COVER: Golden Gate National Recreation Area/Park Archives and Records Center

BACK COVER: John Louie

Chicago Historical Society: p. 16; Roy Eisenhardt: pp. 37, 116; Golden Gate National Recreation Area/Park Archives and Records Center: pp. 5, 7, 9, 15 (Phil Dollison Collection), 21, 31, 38, 42, 54, 59, 70, 84, 92, 97, 101 (b/w), 103, 105, 115, 125 (b/w), 137, 149, 155, 163, 171; Al Greening: pp. 175, 185; Steven Joseph: p. 153; John Louie: pp. 101, 109, 125, 129, 135, 138, 139, 143, 145, 166, 181; San Francisco Public Library/San Francisco History Center: pp. 49, 60, 69, 75, 79; Chuck Stucker collection: p. 58; Brenda Tharp: p. 85.

Poster Credits

Alcatraz Island © Turner Entertainment Co. A Warner Bros. Entertainment Company. All Rights Reserved. Used with permission.

Birdman of Alcatraz © 1962 Metro-Goldwyn-Mayer Studios Inc. All Rights Reserved. Courtesy of MGM CLIP+STILL. Used with permission. Burt Lancaster and related rights: ™© The Burt Lancaster 1988 Revocable Trust, used under license. Represented by The Roger Richman Agency, Inc. Used with permission.

El Gangster y la Bailarina (1940) with George Raft & Joan Bennett. No known copyright holder at this time.

The Enforcer © Warner Bros. Inc./Malpaso. All Rights Reserved. Used with permission.

Escape from Alcatraz © Paramount Pictures/Malpaso. Used with permission.

Experiment Alcatraz © RKO Pictures. Licensed by Warner Bros. Entertainment Inc. All Rights Reserved. Used with permission.

King of Alcatraz © 1938. Courtesy of Universal Studios Licensing LLLP. Used with permission.

The Last Gangster © Turner Entertainment Co. A Warner Bros. Entertainment Company. All Rights Reserved. Used with permission. Edward G. Robinson and related rights © The Edward G. Robinson Estate, used under license. Represented by The Roger Richman Agency. Used with permission.

Murder in the First © Warner Bros., a Division of Time Warner Entertainment Company, L. P. and Le Studio Canal+ (U.S.). All Rights Reserved. Used with permission.

Passport to Alcatraz © 1940, renewed 1968 Columbia Pictures Industries, Inc. All Rights Reserved. Courtesy of Columbia Pictures. Used with permission.

Point Blank © Turner Entertainment Co. A Warner Bros. Entertainment Company. All Rights Reserved. Used with permission of Mrs. Lee Marvin and Angie Dickinson.

The Rock © Hollywood Pictures/Disney. Courtesy Nicolas Cage, Sean Connery, Ed Harris. Used with permission.

San Francisco Docks © 1940. Courtesy of Universal Studios Licensing LLLP. Used with permission.

Seven Miles from Alcatraz © RKO Pictures. Licensed by Warner Bros. Entertainment Inc. All Rights Reserved. Used with permission

Skidoo © Paramount Pictures. Used with permission.

Train to Alcatraz © Paramount Pictures. Used with permission.

"You've got to admit, it's a pretty piece of masonry, that Alcatraz, but it never was a choice spot for a vacation."

Champ Larkin, *Seven Miles from Alcatraz* (1942)

■■■■■■■■■■■

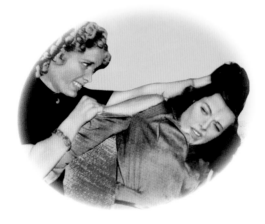

San Francisco Docks, 1941

CONTENTS

FOREWORD

by Rich Weideman, *Chief, Public Affairs*
Golden Gate National Recreation Area, National Park Service

When Alcatraz opened as a federal prison in 1934, it wasn't long before it was popularly known as "America's Devil's Island." Though access was restricted until the island came under the protection of the National Park Service in 1972, many feel they "know" Alcatraz because they have watched one or more of the dozens of films that Hollywood has produced using it as a backdrop.

The earliest Alcatraz movie, made in 1937, was titled simply and directly: *Alcatraz Island*. This film, along with later movies, promised the viewers a look inside the world's most dreaded prison—"the end of the line" for the nation's bad guys. While filmgoers thought they were seeing the inside of Alcatraz, what they were really being given was not only a Hollywood set, but also Hollywood's version of what the Rock was like.

The 1940s continued the story of Alcatraz as a desolate, cold place where hope went to die. Movies like *Train to Alcatraz* and *Seven Miles from Alcatraz* featured desperate men trying to escape their hell on earth: Alcatraz. Alcatraz inmates were trying to escape torture, but not the kind portrayed in the movies. The torture offered by incarceration on Alcatraz was the routine, the boredom, and the total isolation, all within daily view of one of the world's most beautiful cities.

From the 1950s until the prison closed in 1963, movies continued to perpetuate the myth of "Hellcatraz," as the island was often called. The most famous film of this period was *Birdman of Alcatraz* (1962). In this film, not only was Alcatraz a horrible prison, it confined a man portrayed as a fine and gentle soul. In fact, starting with this film, Hollywood has regularly asked audiences to side with mistreated inmates against heartless Alcatraz wardens and prison guards.

After the Rock was closed as a federal prison in 1963, filmmakers were allowed to actually film on location, which might have translated into more accurate movies. However, that was not the case. For example, both *Escape from Alcatraz* (1978) and *Murder in the First* (1995) were filmed primarily on Alcatraz and both portray terrible conditions: uncontrollable inmates, sadistic guards and wardens, and a high level of violence—not to mention walls so weak they could be penetrated with a table spoon and stays in isolation that were measured in years rather than days.

Hollywood, of course, is in the business of mass entertainment, not historical documentation. Enjoy these old Alcatraz movies—and new ones as they're released—for what they are: dramatic stories springing almost entirely from screenwriters' imaginations. For the truth, visit Alcatraz itself.

INTRODUCTION

In the late 1920s and early 1930s, Prohibition and the Great Depression sparked a wave of criminal activity and the rise of crime syndicates. The federal penitentiary on Alcatraz was developed as an antidote to this crime wave. The public was hungry to know who these criminals were, and Hollywood was the perfect vehicle to dramatize their stories. For at least 70 years, in dozens of movies and television productions, Hollywood has used the image and aura of Alcatraz to create its own cinematic mystique.

In movie after movie, Hollywood invoked Alcatraz—the most feared prison in the nation set in one of the most beautiful places in the world—using the island's atmosphere and location to enhance its stories and sell tickets. Who were the studios, filmmakers, stars, and creative talent behind these movies? How did Hollywood help Alcatraz become known as "America's Devil's Island"? What was it like filming on the Rock, or trying to create the notorious prison on a studio back lot? What is the truth behind the fiction?

This book is an exploration and a celebration of the films and filmmakers who helped create the Alcatraz legend.

1937 ··

ALCATRAZ ISLAND

Directed by
WILLIAM C. MCGANN

WARNER BROTHERS
63 minutes, Black and White

CAST

John Litel	Gat Brady
Ann Sheridan	Flo Allen
Mary Maguire	Ann Brady
Gordon Oliver	George Drake
Ben Welden	Red Carroll
Dick Purcell	Harp Santell
Addison Richards	Fred MacLane
George E. Stone	Tough Tony Burke
Vladimir Sokoloff	Dutch
Peggy Bates	Miss "Tolly" Tolliver

CREATIVE

Producer	Bryan Foy
Screenplay	Crane Wilbur
Cinematography	L. William O'Connell
Editing	Frank DeWar
Art Direction	Esdras Hartley
Music	Sanford Green, Heinz Roemheld
Costumes	Howard Shoup

THE STORY

"**K**illing is no part of my racket," declares mob boss Gat Brady when one of his men, Red Carroll, asks him to find a safe hideout for his brother Butch, a hired killer wanted by the police. When the police kill Butch in a shootout, Red blames Brady and vows revenge.

Brady, whose daughter Ann will soon be out of boarding school, wants to keep her away from his underworld life and decides they should move to London with his girlfriend Flo. Before they leave, however, Brady is picked up by the US Attorney General's office on tax-evasion charges. He's quickly found guilty and sentenced to five years in USP Leavenworth.

Red has been waiting for his chance to get even with Brady, and seizes the opportunity to kidnap Ann. The plucky Ann escapes from Red's speeding car, and the police soon catch up with him. Brady is furious about the kidnapping, and when Red shows up at Leavenworth, Brady attacks him, an action that sends Brady to the maximum-security federal penitentiary on Alcatraz Island.

Still out for revenge, Red starts a fight with a guard to get himself transferred to Alcatraz. One day, while the two men are both working in the Alcatraz wood shop, Red is stabbed with Brady's work knife, and with his dying breath, he blames Brady. Accused of murder, Brady could spend the rest of his life on Alcatraz.

Ann and Flo know Brady is innocent, and seek help from DA George Drake, the man responsible for sending Brady to prison in the first place. At first, Drake declines, but Ann is pretty and persistent, and the young Drake falls in love with her and agrees to help. He plants an undercover investigator on Alcatraz, who poses as an inmate and discovers the identity of the real murderer. Brady, now found to be innocent of murder, is soon happily reunited with his family.

"**Wait till you get in your bunk tonight and the siren in the lighthouse begins to moan, when fog settles down over the Bay...just the same as being in your grave, only you miss the fun of being dead.**"

Inmate, *Alcatraz Island* (1937)

PRISON, SOUTHWEST VIEW

THE INSIDE SCOOP

Alcatraz Island is a solid B production, made with Warner's contract actors and creative team, but its landmark distinction is in being the first motion picture in which Alcatraz appears in a film and in a film title. This fame was won by a nose; *Alcatraz Island* reached theaters on November 6, 1937, only a week prior to the second Alcatraz-connected film, *The Last Gangster*, starring Edward G. Robinson. With *Alcatraz Island*, the prison's unique (and ongoing) movie career was launched.

In the early 1930s, Warner Brothers established the gangster genre with a series of films focusing on brutal mobsters, but by the end of the decade, these hard-core criminals had been softened up. The 1937 *Alcatraz Island* presents a "kinder" gangster, one who would never kill anyone, though he has no trouble stealing money. Gat Brady is a businesslike mob boss, soft-spoken, kind to his daughter, and considerate of his girlfriend. By the end of the film, Brady wants to reform, and even gets help from the district attorney who convicted him. Unfortunately, this mild portrayal creates a less-than-sensational story. Litel and Sheridan make a good pair, but it's Ben Weldon as Red, the "bad" criminal, who adds the real spark.

In 1937, Warner Brothers released two prison films starring Ann Sheridan, *Alcatraz Island* and *San Quentin*. Although Alcatraz is the undisputed king of the prison film genre, the real USP Alcatraz was only three years old in 1937; by contrast, San Quentin State Prison—built in response to a crime wave fueled by the throngs of men coming to California in 1848 seeking their fortunes in gold—was more than fifty. Interestingly, *Alcatraz Island* was filmed in a studio re-creation of the prison in LA's San Fernando Valley, and at San Quentin State Prison.

the Gangster studio: **WARNER BROTHERS**

It was fitting that Warner Brothers released the first Alcatraz-themed film—the studio had built its reputation on hard-hitting crime movies, and in so doing, established itself as a major force in the film industry. Throughout the '30s, Warner Brothers was the undisputed master of the gangster genre, a subject that was finally eclipsed when America entered WWII and the international criminal took the spotlight.

Warner Brothers was started in 1918 by brothers Harry, Sam, Albert, and Jack Warner. By the late 1920s, sound had added a new dimension to filmmaking, and the studio jumped on the bandwagon, releasing the groundbreaking movie, *The Jazz Singer* (1927), and many expensive musicals. However, the stock market crash of '29 and the ensuing economic depression affected the movie business as it did everything else. Warner Brothers found itself in serious debt and looking for ways to recover.

The studio's goal was achieved, when, led by the visionary Daryl F. Zanuck and aided by substantial bank loans, it hit gold by using the day's headlines as source material—Americans were living through a financial disaster and the realities of everyday life were of national concern. Energized by its cadre of fast "action" directors and a new group of young, tough actors—among them, James Cagney, Bette Davis, Edward G. Robinson, and Humphrey Bogart—Warner became known as the "working-man's" studio, and its most popular films focused on realism and the underbelly of society.

Warner Brothers' strategy worked well; audiences were interested and profits were high. As running times were trimmed and the line between the longer A-feature films and secondary B-features began to blur, the studio's contract actors followed a busy, six-day-week schedule. The common gangster theme and use of similar urban locations also enabled the studio to save money by using its back lot over and over again.

In 1931, Warner Brothers produced two of its biggest hits, films that propelled the company and defined the gangster genre: *Little Caesar* and *The Public Enemy*. Newcomers Edward G. Robinson and James Cagney shot to stardom.

ALCATRAZ: REEL TO REAL

With the title of the film *Alcatraz Island*, director McGann made sure that the island prison played its part as an unwelcome and menacing character.

The music soars as a view of the island fills the screen, juxtaposed with a headline describing it as a "fortress, grim and mysterious." In the film, Alcatraz is portrayed as a prison where the rules, especially the rule of silence, are strictly enforced: "The screws say if you talk, you'll get ten days in the hole," whispers a prisoner. This rule of silence, though enforced in the prison's early years, was found to be impractical, and by 1937, had been abandoned. Though the punishment may not have been as severe as the screenwriter imagined, the action in *Alcatraz Island* leaves no doubt that the Rock was the toughest "joint" around, a perception that the Federal Bureau of Prisons was only too happy to have reinforced.

As was true for most Alcatraz inmates, Brady and Red are not sentenced directly to Alcatraz, but when they get in trouble at Leavenworth, are sent to the Rock, the only place that can control them.

VIEW OF CELLHOUSE

"America's penal fortress, grim and mysterious as its name—where cold steel and rushing tides protect civilization from its enemies."

Opening line, *Alcatraz Island*

STARRING

JOHN LITEL (Gat Brady) cast in supporting roles throughout his career, is the star of *Alcatraz Island* and gives a strong performance as a man coming up against the consequences of his criminal life as he tries to protect his daughter. As part of the Warner Brothers stock company, both Litel and costar Ann Sheridan were cast in many A and B Hollywood films. The following year, they were teamed in another WB film, *Little Miss Thoroughbred*, Litel again as a gangster and Sheridan as his wife. Litel's acting career spanned more than fifty years and one hundred sixty films and television appearances. Among his many movies for Warner were *The Life of Emile Zola* (1937), *Jezebel* (1938), *Dodge City* (1939), and *They Drive by Night* (1940).

ANN SHERIDAN (Flo Allen) brings considerable glamour to *Alcatraz Island*. Her role as Gat Brady's refined girlfriend suited her beauty and stature. Sheridan came to Hollywood by winning a beauty contest and with it, a Paramount screen test that lead to many small roles at the studio. Sheridan signed with Warner Brothers in 1936, and the studio publicized her as the "Oomph Girl" and a pin-up during WWII. Sheridan played many gangster girlfriends in films throughout the '30s. She was in the hit, *Angels with Dirty Faces* (1938) with Humphrey Bogart and James Cagney, and at Warner Brothers, she starred in *Torrid Zone* and *City for Conquest* (both 1940), *Kings Row* (1942), and *Nora Prentiss* (1947). In 1949, not long after leaving Warner Brothers, she made the 20th Century Fox hit comedy, *I Was a Male War Bride* (1949), directed by Howard Hawks and costarring Cary Grant.

BEN WELDEN (Red Carroll), was the quintessential gangster-type, a persona he played in many Hollywood films from the '30s to the '70s. He was short and round, and his distinctive New York accent captured the essence of the screen villain, often with a comic edge. Welden is best remembered for his portrayals of numerous criminals in the popular '50s *"Adventures of Superman"* TV series. Welden has the distinction of appearing in three Alcatraz films: *Alcatraz Island*, *The Last Gangster* (in which he portrayed a character with the wonderful name of Bottles Bailey, son of Stinky Bailey), and as Bender in *Passport to Alcatraz* (1950).

GORDON OLIVER (George Drake), like Ann Sheridan, had feature roles in two prison films in 1937, *Alcatraz Island* and *San Quentin*. Oliver has appeared in many notable films including *Jezebel* (1938) with Bette Davis, *Brother Rat* (1938) with Ronald Reagan, *Since You Went Away* (1944) with Claudette Colbert, and *The Spiral Staircase* (1946) with Dorothy McGuire and Robert Preston (*King of Alcatraz*). Gordon worked in television in the late 1950's and '60s as Executive Producer of the popular heist series, *It Takes a Thief,* starring Robert Wagner, among other shows.

BEHIND THE SCENES

Director WILLIAM C. McGANN made over fifty B films and shorts for Warner Brothers between 1930 and 1944. McGann's first film, *On the Border* (1930), featured John Litel, and starred Warner Brothers' most successful talent, Rin Tin Tin. McGann worked with many Warner stars, including Humphrey Bogart (*Two Against the World*, 1936), Ronald Reagan (*Girls on Probation*, 1938), and John Garfield (*Blackwell's Island*, 1939). In 1944, McGann stopped directing and began a successful career creating special effects for many of Warner's top features. His special effects work can be seen in *A Stolen Life* (1946, Oscar nomination), *Possessed* (1947), and *The Treasure of Sierra Madre* (1948).

Screenwriter CRANE WILBER is known for his prison films *Crime School* (1938) and *Inside the Walls of Folsom State Prison* (1951), and the crime thrillers *He Walked by Night* (1948) and *The George Raft Story* (1961). Wilber's last effort was another prison film, *House of Women* (1962).

Producer BRIAN FOY grew up on the vaudeville circuit (one of the *"Seven Little Foys"*), and headed the B movie division at Warner Brothers during the '30s. Foy produced *Alcatraz Island* (among other gangster films), as well as the popular "Nancy Drew" series (starring Bonita Granville, *Seven Miles From Alcatraz*). Foy's notable films include *Guadalcanal Diary* (1943), *House of Wax* (1953), and *PT 109* (1963). He received an Oscar nomination for *I Was a Communist for the FBI* (1951), written by Crane Wilber.

Cinematographer L. WILLIAM O'CONNELL worked for six decades on over one hundred and sixty features, second reels, shorts, Shirley Temple films, and serials from the silent-film era to the 1950s. O'Connell worked for many top directors, including Alexander Korda (*Princess and the Plumber*, 1930), Raoul Walsh (*Under Pressure*, 1935), and Howard Hawks on the seminal gangster film *Scarface* (1932).

Editor FRANK DEWAR spent only seven years in Hollywood, where he worked for Warner Brothers editing newsreels, shorts, full-length features, and a number of animal documentaries including *American Saddle Horses* (1939), *Famous Movie Dogs* and *Diary of a Racing Pigeon* (both 1940), and his last film, *Lions for Sale* (1941).

Costume Designer HOWARD SHOUP was hired at Warner Brothers in 1937 and stayed with the studio for thirty years; his last film was the prison drama, *Cool Hand Luke* (1967), starring Paul Newman. He often worked on a number of movies simultaneously—in 1938 alone, he was involved with over twenty films. Shoup's primary responsibility on his first one hundred films was women's gowns, and *Alcatraz Island* has a party scene that shows off his work; Ann Sheridan's gown, in particular, is a knockout. Shoup won five Oscar nominations.

film poster

The words ALCATRAZ ISLAND against prison bars say it all. Though Warner Brothers produced a variety of posters for the film, this version takes full advantage of the prison's infamous name and reputation. USP Alcatraz had only been open for three years when the movie was released, but it had already garnered attention as the toughest prison in America. Al Capone was among the first criminals sent to Alcatraz, and his story made headline news, inspiring a number of Hollywood films of the '30s. The first to use the name "Alcatraz" as a marketing strategy, it grabbed the public's attention, as Warner Brothers knew it would. It's significant that no images of stars Ann Sheridan or John Litel appear, but clearly, the words "Alcatraz Island" and the image of prison bars were enough to market the film and intrigue audiences.

The Belgium version of the poster is titled *L'Ile du Diable* (Devil's Island), a reference to France's notoriously brutal island prison. The French Devil's Island is one of three collectively known as Isles du Salut (Salvation Islands) in French Guiana, which operated as a prison from the mid-1800s until 1953. This reference—"America's Devil's Island"—would be used many times in connection with Alcatraz. Alcatraz's reputation as the icon for tough prisons has gone full circle. Recently, a prison opened on an island off the coast of France was referred to as the "French Alcatraz."

CORRECTIONAL OFFICERS WITH DEPUTY WARDEN CECIL J. SHUTTLEWORTH
IN FRONT OF PRISON ADMINISTRATION BUILDING

THE LAST GANGSTER

Directed by
EDWARD LUDWIG

MGM
81 minutes, Black and White

CAST

Edward G. Robinson	Joe Krozac
James Stewart	Paul North
Rose Stradner	Talya Krozac
Lionel Stander	Curly
Douglas Scott	Paul North, Jr., AKA Joe Krozac, Jr.
John Carradine	Caspar
Sidney Blackmer	San Francisco newspaper editor
Grant Mitchell	Warden
Edward Brophy	Fats Garvey
Alan Baxter	Frankie "Acey" Kile
Frank Conroy	Sid Gorman
Louise Beavers	Gloria

CREATIVE

Producer	Lou L. Ostrow
Story	Robert Carson, William A. Wellman
Screenplay	John Lee Mahin
Cinematography	William H. Daniels
Editing	Ben Lewis
Art Direction	Cedric Gibbons
Music	Edward Ward
Gowns	Adrian

EDWARD G.
ROBINSON
THE LAST GANGSTER
Greatest Thrill Drama Since "Little Caesar"!
WITH James STEWART
ROSE STRADNER
Lionel STANDER
DOUGLAS SCOTT
John CARRADINE
Sidney BLACKMER
SCREEN PLAY BY JOHN LEE MAHIN · ORIGINAL STORY BY WILLIAM A. WELLMAN AND ROBERT CARSON · Directed by EDWARD LUDWIG
A Metro-Goldwyn-Mayer PICTURE
MP1031

THE STORY

Celebrity mob boss Joe Krozac returns to New York from Europe with his new wife Talya, who doesn't speak English and doesn't know how Joe makes his money. When Talya tells Joe she's pregnant, he's exuberant, but his mood quickly changes when he learns that his Brooklyn territory has been taken over by the Kile brothers. Joe orders the murder of all the brothers. He gets back his territory, but the youngest brother, "Acey" Kile survives. Soon after, Joe is issued a federal summons on tax-evasion charges. He's quickly found guilty, and sentenced to ten years in the country's most dreaded prison, Alcatraz.

Talya travels to San Francisco to see Joe with their new baby boy. As she leaves Alcatraz, reporters accost her for information. When a picture of her baby appears on the front of a newspaper, she goes to the paper's offices demanding an explanation. Reporter Paul North and his editor show Talya story after story about Joe's gangster activities. Talya is overwhelmed and breaks down. She begs them not to write about her baby, but the editor knows good copy when he sees it. Paul, who cannot bear to see her being treated so heartlessly, quits on the spot and leaves with Talya.

Talya goes to Alcatraz and tells Joe that she's taking their son away forever. Joe goes wild and screams that he'll find her and he'll kill her and get his son back. Talya, Paul, and the baby move to Boston. Talya divorces Joe, marries Paul, and they raise the child as their own. Joe serves his time, but he must endure abuse by other prisoners who have long been on the receiving end of Joe Krozac's brutality.

After ten years, Joe is released from Alcatraz. He goes to New York to find his son and meet his gang, but things have changed in ten years. The gang only want Joe's money and they torture him to find out where he's hidden it. Joe is fierce and continues to deny he has any. Then, the gang kidnaps Joe's ten-year old son and start to torture the boy. Joe can't stand it, and takes them to a remote area to get the money. The gang abandons Joe and his son, who must make their way to Boston.

Joe tries to convince his son that he's his real father, but the boy doesn't believe him. By the time they reach Paul and Talya's house, Joe realizes that his son is better off without him. As Joe leaves their house, Acey Kile, the brother who survived the killing, is waiting for him. Kile shoots Joe and tells him he's going to expose his son's true identity to the newspapers. Joe is dying, but he lunges at Acey, kills him with his bare hands, and then falls dead in the street.

THE INSIDE SCOOP

The Last Gangster, as its title implies, came at the end of the genre's heyday, but in 1937, criminals were still making headlines and the public was still interested in their stories. They were also keenly interested in stories of a new island prison designed as a maximum-security institution to discipline the worst of America's criminals. Robinson's portrayal of a mob boss played directly into the newspaper accounts of the day, particularly stories of Al Capone (a real Alcatraz inmate), a ruthless gang boss who, like Joe Krozac, could only be convicted on income tax evasion. Alcatraz was a "hot topic," particularly because so little was known about the prison. Its secrecy fed its notorious reputation, and stories about it were purposefully not denied by authorities. Known as the "toughest of the tough," Alcatraz was a Hollywood dream.

CORRECTIONAL OFFICER ON TOWER DUTY

Promoted as "the greatest thrill drama since *Little Caesar*," *The Last Gangster* is a tough-guy film, propelled by the reputation and force of its powerful star, Edward G. Robinson. Robinson became a star playing the brutal mob boss Rico in the classic gangster film *Little Caesar* (1931) and echoes of Rico abound in his performance as Joe Krozac, especially his contempt for authority. In *The Last Gangster*, Joe cannot believe he'll be sent to prison, "I ain't goin' to no federal pen. There isn't one big enough to hold Joe Krozac." In *Little Caesar*, Rico confronts a police officer with, "No buzzard like you will ever put the cuffs on Rico."

Though MGM tried to equate the two films, aside from Robinson's performance, *The Last Gangster* pales in comparison. The six years that separate them saw a sharp change in the gangster genre. *The Last Gangster's* Krozac is still a ruthless mob boss, but he's eventually undermined by the love he has for his son. Though having feelings is something Krozac doesn't expect, this is unlike the irredeemable Rico, who to the end, thinks only of himself—or, as in his final infamous words, "Mother of Mercy! Is this the end of Rico?" The pairing of Robinson and Alcatraz was fitting—the three-year-old prison was headline news and in the public's mind, Robinson was a top gangster, if only a celluloid one.

■ ■ ■ ■ ■ ■ ■ ■ ■ ■ ■

Name: Alphonse Capone
Offense: Violating Income Tax Laws
Date of offense: Oct. 24, 1931
Sentence: 10 years & $37,617.51 fine
Reason for Transfer: Notorious criminal, being a gang leader and racketeer. Suspected of clandestine correspondence while confined at USP Atlanta, and of trying to have money transferred into the institution clandestinely. Transfer is recommended with Close Supervision.

Criminal History: 1919 Arrested-NYC; Disorderly conduct; (Fighting) Discharged. 1923 Arrested-Chicago; Traffic Violation; (Collision) Dismissed. 1923 (Denies) Fined $150; Operating disorderly house; Gambling--- Chicago. 9-5-23-- Arrested with pistol in car; Discharged. 3-5-24-- Arrested-Chicago; witness of murder; Released.1925 Arrested-Olean, NY; Disorderly; Released (Denied)6-7-26-- Indicted-Chicago; Violation of National Prohibition Act. Dismissed 7-15-26-- Indicted-Stickney, IL; Vote fraud; Dismissed 7-28-15-- Arrested-Chicago; Murder; Charge withdrawn 10-1-26-- Indicted-Chicago; Violation of Nat. Prohibition Act (26 others) dismissed 11-12-27-- Arrested-Chicago; Refusal to testify; Dismissed 12-22-27-- Fine $2600, Joliet, IL;(5 other hencmen) Concealed. Weapon 5-17-29 Received at Eastern State Penitentiary, PA Charges: concealed weapon; Discharge by expiration 3-17-30

Escape Attempt: none

Final Whereabouts: Died 1-24-47 from complications brought on by syphilis

the studio: **MGM**

MGM borrowed Robinson from Warner Brothers, the industry's top gangster studio, to star in *The Last Gangster* as Joe Krozac, a fierce mob boss similar to Al Capone, who, like Capone, is sent to Alcatraz for income tax evasion.

MGM was formed in 1924 through a series of mergers, becoming the biggest studio in Hollywood and describing itself as "having more stars than there are in heaven." Its talent included Katherine Hepburn, Spencer Tracy, Clark Gable, Greta Garbo, Joan Crawford, Cary Grant, Gregory Peck, Judy Garland, Jimmy Stewart, Elizabeth Taylor, Gene Kelly, Jean Harlow, and Paul Newman. It was known for producing the highest-quality films in the business. In the '30s alone, MGM's output was astounding: lavish musicals (*The Great Ziegfeld*, 1936; *The Wizard of Oz*, 1939), sensational dramas (*Grand Hotel*, 1932; *Boys Town*, 1938), and historical epics (*San Francisco*, 1936; *Gone with the Wind*, 1939). What MGM was not known for were gangster pictures. Though the studio had success with *The Thin Man* detective series (1934 to 1946), based on Dashiell Hammett's novels, these films were more sophisticated comedies than hard-boiled crime dramas.

The studio brought together the best of its considerable creative team to support Robinson: strong direction by Edward Ludwig, a sharp script by screenwriter John Lee Mahin, beautiful cinematography by William H. Daniels, incisive editing by Ben Lewis, and handsome art direction by Cedric Gibbons.

ALCATRAZ: REEL TO REAL

In 1937, details of life on Alcatraz were not public knowledge, but the cinematic warden, played by Grant Mitchell, gets many of them right in his address to the newly arrived inmates: "During the entire day you will observe the rule of strict silence. In a week or two you will be assigned to the workshops for a morning and afternoon period. Conversations in the yard are allowed only in connection to the work at hand. Recreation and exercise period comes once a week, Saturday, two hours in the yard, but this, of course, depends upon your deportment. If these rules are not obeyed, we have discipline to help you obey."

Though the prison interior appears in numerous scenes, the only scenes incorporating the real Alcatraz were shot from the water (apparent in the up-and-down motion of the island); "civilian" boats could circle the island at a distance, but could not land.

The judge sentences Joe Krozac directly to Alcatraz when, in fact, the prison only accepted convicts other penitentiaries couldn't handle. Though there were exceptions, these were rare. Al Capone, among the first prisoners sent to Alcatraz, was transferred there from USP Atlanta.

The film is set in 1927. In fact, the federal prison on Alcatraz didn't open until 1934.

"I ain't goin' to no federal pen. There isn't one big enough to hold Joe Krozac."

Edward G. Robinson as Joe Krozac, *The Last Gangster*

STARRING

EDWARD G. ROBINSON (Joe Krozac) is ideally cast as celebrity gangster Joe Krozac, a coldblooded man with little feeling for anyone, including his new wife. It's Krozac's son who inspires conflict in the character and brings out Robinson's vibrant performance.

A GANGSTER ICON

Born Emmanuel Goldberg in 1893, Robinson was a small, stocky, forceful man who starred in over ninety Hollywood films. In 1927, Robinson first gained notice on Broadway, playing an Al Capone-type character about the time the real Capone was making headlines. He received great reviews and was courted by movie studios (MGM purportedly offered him a three-year, $1 million contract), but he decided to remain independent. When his Broadway luck changed, he went back to Hollywood at a time when Warner Brothers was hiring a new crop of tough, streetwise talent, including James Cagney and Joan Blondell.

Robinson signed a thousand-dollar weekly contract at Warner, but after disappointing box-office results from his first film (*The Widow of Chicago*, 1930), he was offered a small role in his next film. He brazenly went to the studio and said that he'd only play the lead. Robinson got the part and a chance to play Rico Bandello in the smash hit *Little Caesar*. The critics were unanimous in their evaluation of Robinson's performance, lauding it as one of epic proportion; his merciless killer marked a bold change in the gangster persona. After his rise to stardom in *Little Caesar*, Robinson made fifteen films before *The Last Gangster*. These included the powerful drama, *Five Star Final* (1931); the screwball gangster comedy, *The Whole Town's Talking* (1935); and the boxing movie, *Kid Galahad* (1937). Though Robinson wanted to move away from gangster roles, and was negotiating a new contract with Warner that also gave him script approval and promised him top co-stars, it was at his request that Warner Brothers loaned him to MGM for *The Last Gangster*, to play another gangster with a cast of new talent. He later admitted that he had been upset at his studio, and needed money for his art collection and home remodeling.

Among his more than ninety films were *The Sea Wolf* (1941), *Double Indemnity* (1944), *Scarlet Street* (1945), *All My Sons* (1948), *The Ten Commandments* (1956), and *The Cincinnati Kid* (1965). Though gangsters accounted for only a small number of Robinson's performances, his persona as a fierce mob boss could not be overshadowed, and along with James Cagney, George Raft, and Humphrey Bogart, he was part of an elite group of major stars who became the icons of the film gangster.

JIMMY STEWART (Paul North) received second billing in *The Last Gangster*, his eleventh film. The soon-to-be famous Stewart was being groomed by MGM for stardom, and his character Paul North, the jaded reporter turned idealistic small town newspaperman, foreshadows many of his future good-guy roles. Stewart plays the part well, but his role is secondary and never a strong foil for Robinson. *The Last Gangster* was released two years before Stewart's star-making performance as a naïve senator who brings down congressional corruption in Frank Capra's *Mr. Smith Goes to Washington* (1939). Ultimately, Stewart became one of the most admired and loved actors of all time, with a long career punctuated by some of the century's most celebrated films, including *The Philadelphia Story* (1940), *It's a Wonderful Life* (1946), *Call Northside 777* (1948), *Harvey* (1950), *Rear Window* (1954), *Vertigo* (1958), and *Anatomy of a Murder* (1959).

ROSE STRADNER (Talya) was an Austrian actress discovered by Louis B. Mayer in Europe while searching for new talent. *The Last Gangster* was Stradner's first and only starring vehicle. Stradner married illustrious film producer, writer, and director Joseph L. Mankiewicz in 1939 (unusual in Hollywood, they remained married until her death in 1958). Stradner's only other significant role was in Mankiewicz's 1944 drama, *Keys to the Kingdom*, starring Gregory Peck.

JOHN CARRADINE'S (Casper) tall, gaunt presence graced over two hundred and fifty films. He gives a wonderfully eccentric performance in *The Last Gangster* as a crazed Alcatraz con out to get Robinson. His films include *Captains Courageous* (1937), *Stagecoach* (1939), *The Grapes of Wrath* (1940), and *The Ten Commandments* (1956). He is remembered for his many horror films, including *House of Frankenstein and Billy the Kid versus Dracula* (both 1944), and *Doom of Dracula* (1966). He is the father of actors Keith and David Carradine.

LIONEL STANDER'S (Curly) gravelly voice and tough-guy looks were effective in both dramas and comedies. Stander gets a few choice lines in *The Last Gangster*, and makes the most of them. Stander made over fifty films in the '30s and '40s, including *Mr. Deeds Goes to Town* (1936), *A Star is Born* (1937), and *Guadalcanal Diary* (1943). In 1951, falling victim to the McCarthy/HUAC "witch hunt," Stander (one of the most courageous and vocal opponents of the HUAC) went to Europe and worked in Italian films, including Sergio Leone's masterpiece *Once Upon a Time in the West* (1968). He later had a successful television career.

LOUISE BEAVERS (Gloria) was one of the first African American film stars. Though often relegated to playing a maid or cook, Beavers appeared in more than one hundred and fifty films over a span of seventy years. Her films included *What Price Hollywood* (1932), *She Done Him Wrong* (1933), *Mr. Blandings Builds His Dream House* (1948), and *The Jackie Robinson Story* (1950). In 1934, Beavers starred opposite Claudette Colbert in *Imitation of Life*, exploring racial prejudice.

PRISON, SOUTHEAST VIEW, FROM WATER

"There she is, boys. You're gonna snuggle in the arms of Alcatraz. If you ever hear a tougher story, it's when you step out of your coffin".

The Last Gangster

BEHIND THE SCENES

Director EDWARD LUDWIG was twenty-four when he made his first picture, a silent Western titled *The Man Who Waited* (1922). Russian-born and American-educated, Ludwig spent his early years at Universal Studios, writing and directing dozens of silent comedy shorts. After a few feature films at Universal, he worked at many of the major studios directing dramas, musicals, adventures, and action films. Ludwig's films were mostly second features, but among his more notable efforts were *Adventure in Manhattan* (1936), *Swiss Family Robinson* (1940), and *The Fighting Seabees* (1944). In *The Last Gangster*, Ludwig creates an entertaining gangster film, taking advantage of Robinson's charged charisma and a colorful script by John Lee Mahin. In 1957, Ludwig went back to his original genre and started a career in television Westerns, directing episodes of *The Restless Gun* (1957), *The Texan* (1958), *Bonanza* (1959), and *Branded* (1965).

Writers ROBERT CARSON and **WILLIAM WELLMAN** created the original story for *The Last Gangster*. The interesting premise explores the downfall of a mob boss caused not by a bullet (though he does die by one), but ultimately by the love he has for his son. Krozac is a maniacal gangster who is also human, redeemed by compassion. The year *The Last Gangster* was released, Wellman and Carson's story for *A Star is Born* won an Oscar. Carson's writing career included screenplays for Wellman's *Beau Geste* (1939), and Fritz Lang's *Western Union* (1941). Wellman had a long directing career, including the classic gangster film, *Public Enemy* (1931). Known as *"Wild Bill"* for his hostile directing style (and fondness for alcohol), Wellman was at the helm of such classic films as *A Star is Born* (1937), *The Lady of Burlesque* (1943), and *The Ox Bow Incident* (1943)

Screenwriter JOHN LEE MAHIN had a prolific career as one of Hollywood's top writers. Mahn's dialogue in *The Last Gangster* is both witty and mean, and the cast, especially Robinson and Stander, make the most of it. Describing Alcatraz for the first time, Mahin writes, "There she is, boys. You're gonna snuggle in the arms of Alcatraz. If you ever hear a tougher story, it's when you step out of your coffin." Mahin was nominated for a Best Screenplay Oscar for *Captains Courageous* (1937), and again in 1957 for *Heaven Knows, Mr. Allison* (1957).

Cinematographer WILLIAM H. DANIELS was known for his skill at creating distinctive visual atmospheres, developed when working on Eric Von Stroheim's early films while still in his twenties. Director of photography at Universal, he went with Stroheim to MGM in 1922, and two years later, was the lead cinematographer for Stroheim's *Greed* (1924). Daniels' career at MGM (1924 to 1943) included being Greta Garbo and Norma Shearer's favorite cameraman. His film credits include *Grand Hotel* (1932), *Dinner at Eight* (1933), *Camille* (1936), and *Marie Antoinette* (1938). Daniels was nominated for three Oscars and in 1949, took home the prize for his gritty black-and-white work on *The Naked City*. Considered one of the great Hollywood cinematographers, Daniels established particularly evocative lighting effects for *The Last Gangster*, especially in scenes set inside the fictional Alcatraz.

Editor BEN LEWIS started his career as one of the editors of the great silent classic, *Ben Hur* (1925) starring Ramon Navarro. Lewis worked at MGM from their early reign as Hollywood's most prestigious studio to their later waning years. During his career he edited some of their most popular and successful films including many of the *Andy Hardy* series, *Tarzan the Ape Man* (1932), *Dinner at Eight* (1933), *Manhattan Melodrama* (1934), and *Lassie Come Home* (1943).

Art Director CEDRIC GIBBONS is acknowledged as the most influential art director in the history of film. During his thirty-two-year reign at MGM, he oversaw more than one thousand films and personally art directed at least one hundred and fifty of them, including *The Last Gangster*. Gibbons created and maintained the MGM style, from glorious black-and-white through its shift to glossy color, setting the standard for the movie industry. He not only won eleven Oscars and thirty-nine nominations, he is credited with designing the Oscar statuette.

Composer EDWARD WARD was a seven-time Oscar nominee and wrote a robust crime score for *The Last Gangster*. Characteristic of many early Alcatraz films, whenever the dreaded prison appears on-screen, the music soars in a dramatic crescendo, as the ominous island's rocky shores signal tough times ahead. Working mostly at MGM and Universal Studios, his movies include *Mannequin* (1937), *Boys Town* (1938), *The Women* (1939), *Cheers for Miss Bishop* (1941), and *Phantom of the Opera* (1943).

film poster

MGM was well known for its exceptional advertising, but *The Last Gangster* was not a great effort. The poster's design, jammed with copy and pictures of the stars, lacks imagination. Relying on Edward G. Robinson's reputation, the poster is dominated by his image and name. The typeface is more ghostly then gangster, and the film's subtitle, *"The Greatest Thrill Drama Since Little Caesar,"* lacks conviction. Robinson's green-skinned portrait misses the character's sophisticated lifestyle, willful energy, and Alcatraz prison story. Contractual agreements often affected the focus of promotional posters; in the '30s, stars had significant control over how their image and name were presented, both in size and placement. There's no mistaking that this is an Edward G. Robinson film.

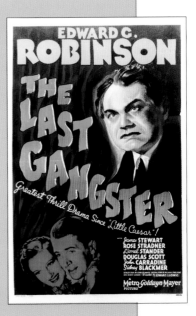

KING OF ALCATRAZ

Directed by
ROBERT FLOREY

PARAMOUNT
68 minutes, Black and White

CAST

Gail Patrick	Dale Borden
Lloyd Nolan	Raymond Grayson
Robert Preston	Robert MacArthur
J. Carrol Naish	Steve Murkil
Harry Carey	Captain Glennan
Anthony Quinn	Lou Gedney
Dennis Morgan	First mate Rogers
Porter Hall	Mathew Talbot
Richard Denning	Harry Vay
Konstantin Shayne	Murok
Edie Marr	Dave Carter
Emory Parnell	Olaf
Paul Fix	"Nails" Miller
Virginia Vale	Dixie

CREATIVE

Producer	William Thomas
Screenplay	Irving Reis
Cinematography	Harry Fischbeck
Editing	Eda Warren
Art Direction	Hans Dreier, A. Earl Hedrick
Stock Music	Gerard Barbonara
	Frederick Hollander
	Milan Roder

Escape!
FROM ALCATRAZ!
PIRACY
ON THE
HIGH SEAS!
KING OF
ALCATRAZ
with
LLOYD NOLAN
GAIL PATRICK
J. CARROL NAISH
HARRY CAREY ★ PORTER HALL

THE STORY

On San Francisco's wharf, two virile wireless operators, Ray Grayson and Bob MacArthur, clash once again in a drunken brawl over the same women. Their continual fights force their captain to reassign them from their luxury ship to an unpretentious freighter, the SS *Escobar Vagabond*. A few passengers join the crew, including an elderly woman accompanied by male attendants, and Nurse Dale Borden, who is quickly spotted by both Ray and Bob. Ray and Dale were once romantically involved, and though things didn't work out, it's easy to see they still love each other. Bob is also crazy about Dale, but has stayed away until now. The men curse their luck, to be on board with the one woman they both truly love.

Later that night, as the *Escobar* sails into the high seas, word comes across the wireless that Steve Murkil, Public Enemy Number 1, has escaped from Alcatraz. He was last spotted on San Francisco's wharf, from which the *Escobar* had set sail. Captain Glennen asks all passengers to show their passports. When the old woman and her escorts present their passports, "Grandma" turns out to be none other than a disguised Steve Murkil, and the escorts, his mob. They quickly take over and force Ray and Bob to radio authorities that all's clear, and that Steve Murkil is not on the ship. As night descends, the *Escobar* heads off course to a safe foreign port.

Ray and Bob cannot stand by while the Murkil mob takes over, and they jump the two thugs guarding them. Ray escapes, but Bob is shot in the arm and recaptured. The gangsters find Ray and bring him back to the wireless room, where Nurse Borden sees that he's dying from a gunshot wound. Bob is the only person who can operate the wireless, so he blackmails Murkil, refusing to respond to incoming messages unless he's allowed to wire a doctor to help Ray. Murkil has no choice, and agrees. Bob finds a doctor aboard another ship, who transmits delicate operating procedures via Morse code. Bob translates the code to Nurse Borden, who successfully performs an intricate surgery. Bob devises a way to send an SOS signal over the wireless. Others on board have their own plans, leading to an explosive ending.

Escape FROM ALCATRAZ! PIRACY ON THE HIGH SEAS!

THE INSIDE SCOOP

Energetically directed by Robert Florey, with a cast of up-and-coming stars, *King of Alcatraz* is a first-rate B feature. The story is tough, the dialogue fast, and there's plenty of rough-and-tumble action. Preston and Nolan are particularly entertaining as the film's sparring heroes, and Naish, as dangerous mob boss Murkil, seems to be having a ball in his "Grandma" disguise. One of the most entertaining scenes is watching Gail Patrick perform an operation on Lloyd Nolan while being given instructions via Morse code (only in Hollywood!). B pictures offered many young actors an opportunity to be cast in a Hollywood movie, even if their screen time is limited, and it's great to see these performers before they became famous. In *King of Alcatraz*, Anthony Quinn (23, in his 17th film) and Dennis Morgan (30, in his 11th film) both play small roles (Quinn a gangster, Morgan the ship's First Mate). Robert Preston was given a lead role in the film, his first. The studio was willing to take a chance on featuring him in this B production, as Preston, a talented performer with a vibrant personality, was well suited to Florey's spirited film style.

Paramount was producing fewer gangster films by the late 1930s, but it had not given up on the genre completely. The studio's considerable contract talent—both in front of and behind the scenes—enabled them to release a steady string of strong B-list gangster films, including *Manslaughter* (1930), *Ladies of the Big House* (1931), *Four Hours to Kill* and *Mary Burns, Fugitive* (both 1935), and Robert Florey's rousing *King of the Gamblers* (1937) and *King of Alcatraz* (1938).

the studio: PARAMOUNT

In the early days of filmmaking, Paramount was Hollywood's biggest and most successful movie studio. In 1916, Adolf Zukor merged his Famous Players with a company run by Jesse Lasky, Cecil B. DeMille, and Samuel Goldwyn. Zukor took charge, making Lasky vice-president and DeMille director general. Goldwyn was forced out (and eventually formed MGM). Zukor ran the studio like a factory, and at its height, it released over one hundred films a year. Paramount's early silent movies featured screen legends Mary Pickford, Douglas Fairbanks, Fatty Arbuckle, and Gloria Swanson.

Zukor built Paramount at a rapid pace, encumbering it with large debts that forced it into bankruptcy when the Depression hit. By 1935, they had restructured, however, and when films went from silent to "talkies," Paramount had an impressive roster of contract stars, including Gary Cooper, W. C. Fields, Mae West, Claudette Colbert, Bing Crosby, Marlene Dietrich, and Bob Hope. The studio also benefited from a cadre of strong directors led by Cecil B. DeMille and including Joseph von Sternberg, Victor Flemming, Leo McCarey, and Ernest Lubtich.

Since its opening in 1934, USP Alcatraz had been heavily promoted as escape-proof. *King of Alcatraz* is noteworthy as the first film in which someone escapes from the prison, a fact heavily publicized in its advertising campaign. However, the way mob boss Steve Murkil gets away is significant—rather than actually escaping off the island, he fakes being ill and makes a break for it while being escorted from Alcatraz to a mainland hospital. This would not have happened to a prisoner on the Rock, as Alcatraz had its own hospital. Nonetheless, his escape makes headline news in the film, and great copy for the poster. (Interestingly, in three of the next four Alcatraz-related films, one or more characters escapes from the island.)

Though there are no scenes of the island, mob boss Murkil is suggestive of Al Capone, who was well known by the public and was incarcerated on the island when the film was released.

THE MODERN GANGSTER FILM

The modern film gangster began at Paramount with the release of the silent film *Underworld* (1927) by thirty-three-year-old Joseph von Sternberg and first-time screenwriter Ben Hecht, who won an Oscar for best original story. Hecht based his story about a criminal gang on his experiences as a Chicago newspaper reporter during Prohibition. The film was a huge hit, and five months later, Paramount released *The City Gone Wild*. They continued in the gangster genre in 1928, releasing *Ladies of the Mob*, starring box-office sensation Clara Bow, the "It Girl"; *The Street of Sin*; *The Racket* (an Oscar nominee for best picture); and *The Drag Net*. In 1929 Sternberg's first talkie, *Thunderbolt* (1929) with Fay Wray, capped the decade. Unfortunately, these subsequent gangster films proved less successful than *Underworld*, and by 1930, Paramount's interest in the genre waned just as Warner Brothers began to build its reputation as the "gangster studio."

STARRING

LLOYD NOLAN (Raymond Grayson) starred in two Alcatraz films, *King of Alcatraz* and as a deceitful lawyer in *House Across the Bay* (1940). In *King of Alcatraz*, Nolan is great as a brawling seaman—lighthearted, lovesick, and tough, fighting the bad guys and winning the girl. Born in San Francisco, Nolan was thirty-six and a veteran of twenty-two films when he made *King of Alcatraz*. His career spanned six decades, ending with a robust performance at age eighty-four in Woody Allen's film *Hannah and Her Sisters* (1986).

ROBERT PRESTON (Robert MacArthur) made his film debut in *King of Alcatraz* at the age of twenty, introducing audiences to his now-familiar animated personality. Preston's career includes his celebrated turn as Professor Howard Hill in *The Music Man* (1962), and his Oscar-nominated performance as Carroll Todd in *Victor Victoria* (1982). A great showman, Preston was also adept at serious roles in the films *This Gun for Hire* (1942), *The Macomber Affair* (1947), and *Dark at the Top of the Stairs* (1960).

GAIL PATRICK (Dale Borden) was often cast as a spoiled rich girl, playing many second leads in comedies of the '30s and '40s. Her statuesque appearance and sultry voice worked particularly well in *My Man Godfrey* (1936), *Stage Door* (1937), and *My Favorite Wife* (1940). It's especially fun watching her play against type as the humble Nurse Borden in *King of Alcatraz*. Patrick left Hollywood in 1948 and became executive producer of the hit courtroom drama *Perry Mason* (1957–66).

J. CARROL NAISH (Steve Murkil) is winning as a tough, sly mob boss who escapes from the Rock. He is equally delightful in full drag as a sweet, gun-toting grandmother. A master of dialect, throughout his career, Naish was cast as Italian, Latin, Arabic, Chinese, Japanese, Jewish, or Indian, but never as the Irishman he truly was. Naish received two Oscar nominations for Best Supporting Actor: *Sahara* (1943) and *A Medal for Benny* (1945).

HARRY CAREY (Captain Glennan) was a celebrated character actor whose career began in 1909 in Bill Sharkey's *Last Game*, directed by D. W. Griffith for the Biograph Company (America's first film company, established in 1895). Carey was called a "$5-per-day" actor. These were people with no acting experience who waited outside the studio for work, and when they got it, were paid $5 a day. As the medium developed, Carey became more established, appearing in close to two hundred silent movies. Many were short (rarely more than seventeen minutes) with small casts, and Carey occasionally directed or wrote the stories. He easily made the transition to talkies, appearing in another sixty-eight films, including his endearing Oscar-nominated performance as Speaker of the House in *Mr. Smith Goes to Washington* (1939).

"Don't try to pull anything, because if you do, I'll break every bone in your heads and toss what's left of you to the sharks."

Captain Glennan, *King of Alcatraz*

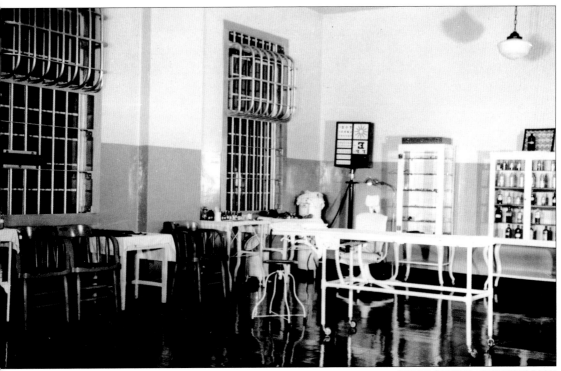

PRISON HOSPITAL, OUTPATIENT ROOM

BEHIND THE SCENES

Director ROBERT FLOREY was a prominent filmmaker known for his sharp, stylish movies. Florey joined Paramount in 1929 after garnering attention for his short film, *The Life and Death of 9413: A Hollywood Extra* (1928), about the dehumanizing nature of the movie business (filmed by legendary cinematographer Greg Toland of *Citizen Kane* fame). Florey made a handful of films at Paramount, including *The Coconuts* (1929), the first Marx Brothers movie; for this extravaganza, he invented the geometric, synchronized dance shot filmed from above (often erroneously attributed to Busby Berkley). He left the United States for two years to work in his native France, then returned to work at Universal Studios, where he first helped write the script for *Frankenstein* (1931) and then directed Bela Lugosi in the classic Gothic horror film, *Murders in the Rue Morgue* (1932). Florey signed with Warner Brothers in 1933, and directed Barbara Stanwyck, Mary Astor, and Bette Davis in some of their lesser-known movies. When Florey arrived back at Paramount in 1935, the Depression had taken its toll on business—the studio was cutting back on the number of yearly productions, but increasing the quality of each film.

Florey was among a group of mostly foreign-born directors (including Josef von Sternberg and Ernest Lubitsch) who helped shape the Paramount style. These directors involved themselves in many aspects of the production. As both a director and art director, Florey turned in some of the classiest movies of the period, taking standard stories, talented contract players and craftspeople, and small budgets

31

and creating sharp and lively movies. By the end of the '30s, Florey was unhappy with directing B movies at Paramount and left to work at other studios. Following his movie days, he built a successful career in the burgeoning small screen, winning television's first Directors Guild Award in 1953 for *The Lost Voyage*. His television work included directing episodes of *Alfred Hitchcock Presents* (1955), *The Twilight Zone* (1959), *The Untouchables* (1959), and *The Outer Limits* (1963).

Screenwriter IRVING REIS started his Hollywood writing career after a short stint as a cinematographer and before becoming a first-rate director. Reis wrote three movies for Paramount in 1938 and '39, but his career took off at RKO, where he began directing films that included *The Big Street* (1942), *Crack-Up* (1946), the Oscar-winning *The Bachelor and the Bobby Soxer* (1947), and *All My Sons* (1948, with Edward G. Robinson). Reis died an untimely death from cancer at 46.

Cinematographer HARRY FISCHBECK was one of the pioneers in the film business, starting in 1914 on the silent film *Life's Shop Window* for a small studio called Box Office Attractions. Fischbeck's first two film assignments for Paramount were to photograph movie heartthrob Rudolf Valentino in *Monsieur Beaucaire* and *A Sainted Devil* (both 1924). His last, *Parole Fixer* (1940), was another Robert Florey "programmer" based on J. Edgar Hoover's book, *Persons in Hiding*.

Editor EDA WARREN began working at Paramount in 1927 at the age of 24 and continued with the studio into the late '50s. As part of Paramount's impressive create team, Warren edited films in many genres. Warren's work can be seen in *Anything Goes* (1936), *The General Died at Dawn* (1936), *I Married a Witch* (1942), *Son of Paleface* (1952), *Pony Express* (1955), *World Strategic Air Command* (1955), *Without End* (1956), and *The Young Savages* (1961).

Art Directors HANS DREIER and **EARL HEDRICK** brought their considerable talents to create the high-seas world in *King of Alcatraz*. German-born Dreier came to Paramount in 1923. For over thirty years, Dreier helped shape Paramount's sophisticated look, and built one of the most prestigious art departments in Hollywood. He received twenty Academy Award nominations and three statues, including one for Gloria Swanson's grand comeback film, *Sunset Boulevard* (1950). Dreier was known for hiring and encouraging talented designers, including Earl Hedrick, who joined the studio in 1932. Dreier and Hedrick's films together include *Sullivan's Travels* (1941), *The Lost Weekend* (1945), *Sorry, Wrong Number* (1948), and *Fancy Pants* (1950).

film poster

Along with their roster of top stars, Paramount, under Adolph Zukor's leadership, developed one of the leading art departments in the business, with Zukor often taking a personal role in approving movie posters. In the 1920s, Vincent Trotta and Maurice Kallis ran Paramount's art department. Artists were rarely allowed to sign their work so most of their talent went unrecognized. Paramount's creative team included well-known illustrators Harrison Fisher, Tony Sarg, and John Held Jr. In 1930, illustrator Herman Heyer became Paramount's chief poster artist, with other leading illustrators from the '30s and '40s, including Miguel Covarrubias, Russell Patterson, George Petty, McLelland Barclay, Rolf Armstrong, and John La Gatta.

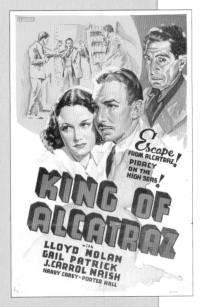

The beautifully illustrated poster for *King of Alcatraz* keeps the film's romantic storyline front and center amidst the threatening presence of gangsters and guns. Exceptionally well-rendered likenesses of film stars Gail Patrick, Lloyd Nolan, and J. Carrol Naish dominate the poster. Robert Preston's image and name do not even appear, though his role has screen-time and significance equal to Nolan's. This was Preston's first film, and he had neither the audience recognition nor studio clout to demand star billing.

Though the island prison never makes an appearance in the film, the importance of the word "Alcatraz" as a marketing tool is evident in the bold three-dimensional letters that dominate the poster's lower section. Worth mentioning is the compelling promotional copy, "Escape From Alcatraz!" appearing above the title. The phrase makes its debut here, suggesting danger and intrigue for the young couple and starting a trend that will be carried into movies for decades to come, most notably forty years later as the title of Clint Eastwood's *Escape from Alcatraz* (1979).

HOUSE ACROSS THE BAY

Directed by
ARCHIE MAYO

UNITED ARTISTS/
WALTER WANGER PRODUCTIONS
88 minutes, black and white

CAST

George Raft	Steve Larwitt
Joan Bennett	Brenda Bentley
Lloyd Nolan	Slant Kolma
Walter Pidgeon	Tim Nolan
Gladys George	Mary Bogel
Billy Wayne	Barney, bartender
June Knight	Bebe
Peggy Shannon	Alice
Max Wagner	Jim
Frank Bruno	Jerry
Joe Sawyer	Charlie
Joesph Crehan	Federal Man
Edward Fielding	Federal Judge
James Craig	Brenda's Friend

CREATIVE

Producer	Walter Wanger
Story	Myles Connolly
Screenplay	Kathryn Scola
Cinematography	Merritt B. Gerstad
Editing	Dorothy Spencer
Lyricist	Nick Castle
Art Direction	Alexander Golitzen
Set Decoration	Julia Heron
Music	Irving Actman, George R. Brown
	Sidney Clare, Werner Janssen
	Al Siegel, Jule Styne
Costumes	Irene
Stunt Pilot	Paul Mantz

PRESENTA A

CEBGSA

George y Joan
RAFT BENNETT

en

El GANGSTER y
la BAILARINA

CON Walter y Lloyd
DIRECTOR PIDGEON NOLAN
ARCHIE MAYO

UNITED ARTISTS

"GRAFICAS VALENCIA" VALENCIA

THE STORY

Sparks fly when nightclub owner Steve Larwitt meets showgirl Brenda Bentley. Fast-talking Brenda is both beautiful and smart, and it doesn't take long for Steve to fall head-over-heels, and the couple soon marry.

Steve expands into racetracks and gunrunning, and his empire flourishes. He lavishes Brenda with diamonds, furs, and a luxurious lifestyle. When Steve sets his sights on a legitimate business owned by a rival gang, he becomes the target of a murder attempt. Brenda fears for his safety and goes to Steve's lawyer, Slant, for advice. They devise a plan that will land Steve in jail for income tax evasion; Slant assures Brenda that Steve will get no more than a year in prison, where he'll be safe while things cool down. The authorities pick up Steve, but during his trial, Slant—who has his eye on Brenda—double-crosses him. Steve is found guilty and sentenced to ten years on Alcatraz.

Brenda moves to San Francisco, taking an apartment with a view of the Rock, and visits Steve every week. One evening, Brenda literally bumps into Tim Nolan, a famous plane designer, who is immediately smitten with Brenda. Brenda does her best to resist, but over time, Nolan wears her down and she starts to enjoy their time together. Slant, who has been having Brenda followed, comes to San Francisco when he finds out about Tim; he tells Brenda that she and Steve are out of money, then declares his love for her. When Brenda becomes angry and rebukes his advances, Slant turns on her and threatens to tell Steve about her two-timing.

Brenda stops seeing Tim and gets a job singing at a nightclub across the bay, in Alameda. Tim finds out where she works and when he goes to see her, Slant catches them together and becomes enraged. He gets a special lawyer's dispensation to see Steve on Alcatraz, and tells him about Brenda and Tim.

Steve is heartbroken, but his hurt quickly turns to anger and that night, he escapes from Alcatraz, swims to San Francisco, highjacks a car, and drives to Alameda. Steve confronts Brenda, and is so upset that he goes out of control and starts to strangle her. Tim walks in and stops him, telling Steve that Brenda has always been faithful, and that Slant double-crossed them both. Steve comes to his senses, and he and Brenda plan to meet later that night in Union Square after he gets money from Slant.

Steve goes to Slant and kills him on the spot. Realizing that Brenda is better off with Tim, Steve takes the car back where he stole it from and swims toward Alcatraz, making himself visible to the armed guard boats patrolling the bay looking for him. Brenda is waiting for Steve in Union Square when she hears a newspaper boy shout, "Gangster Steve Larwitt is dead!"

THE INSIDE SCOOP

From its beautiful opening title sequence—a beam from the Alcatraz lighthouse (the first lighthouse on the West Coast) sweeps across the screen, illuminating the names of the film and its stars—to its dramatic ending, *House Across the Bay* is the best of the early Alcatraz films. Set in the criminal world, it is first and foremost a love story, and Raft and Bennett make an engaging screen couple. Some of the film's best moments are the romantic ones: Raft's awkward proposal in a parking lot, joking together after a night on the town, and parting when Raft is sent to Alcatraz. Unfortunately, Raft spends the second half of the film on Alcatraz and we see him only occasionally in the prison's visiting room. The film misses his energy and the couple's chemistry; the Bennett/Pidgeon connection lags in comparison. (Dapper aircraft designer Howard Hughes, who was also a Hollywood producer [*Scarface,* 1932], and was known to have a way with women, may have inspired Walter Pidgeon's character, Tim Nolan.) Luckily, Gladys George appears in the San Francisco segment as a fellow "Rock" widow, and sparks things up. *House Across the Bay* is noteworthy for the number of top women working behind the scenes including editor Dorothy Spencer, screenwriter Kathryn Scola, and Set Decorator Julia Heron, who helped to create this top-rate production.

House Across the Bay was the first film to take advantage not only of the prison's notorious reputation, but also, its unusual location in the middle of San Francisco Bay. As we watch Bennett and Pidgeon walk the hills of San Francisco and fly over the Golden Gate Bridge and Alcatraz, the irony of the prison's setting amidst abundant natural beauty and urban energy is clearly conveyed. (Film master Alfred Hitchcock—though uncredited—directed Bennett and Pidgeon in these outdoor San Francisco scenes.) For the film's lovers, the Rock is the wall that stands between them, especially poignant as we watch Joan Bennett stare longingly out of her Nob Hill apartment window at the mysterious and sinister island and its house of forgotten men.

ALCATRAZ ISLAND, NORTHERN VIEW FROM WATER

In *House Across the Bay*, plane designer Tim Nolan (Walter Pidgeon) takes Brenda Bentley (Joan Bennet) flying from Crissy Field over the Golden Gate Bridge and Alcatraz. This aerial photograph, circa 1935, of Crissy Field (and the soon to be completed Golden Gate Bridge) offers a spectacular birds-eye-view of the area's dramatic setting. A small airstrip on the northern bayfront of the Presidio of San Francisco, Crissy Field was one of the earliest Army Air Service facilities on the West Coast. Crissy Field saw its share of dashing aviators, as well as dramatic feats of derring-do, and even a few aviation milestones. Today, Crissy Field is a spectacular shoreline park with a restored tidal marsh, shoreline dunes, and historic landmarks.

the studio: UNITED ARTISTS

United Artists was founded in 1919 by director D. W. Griffith, and film stars Mary Pickford, Douglas Fairbanks, and Charlie Chaplin. Their intent was to create a studio where the interests of filmmakers (as opposed to studio chiefs) would be protected. Before United Artists, the rapid growth of the film industry led to mergers and deals wherein the money-men called the shots. Talent, though necessary, shared in neither the wealth nor the artistic decisions. United Artists, which functioned almost exclusively as a distribution entity rather than a production facility, led the way for independents, becoming a breeding ground for creativity and supporting projects that other studios might consider too risky. Gangster films were not among United Artist's usual releases, though they scored big with Howard Hawks' *Scarface* (1932) and *You Only Live Once* (1937), directed by Fritz Lang and produced by Walter Wanger.

ALCATRAZ: REEL TO REAL

Like other movies before and after, the film company did not have access to the island, and the visitor meeting rooms as imagined by Hollywood are on a grand scale, richly embellished with high ceilings and dramatic lighting and dramatized by shadows from prison bars.

Though in reality, Alcatraz was for convicts whom other federal prisons couldn't control or wanted to isolate, in the film, Larwitt is sent directly to Alcatraz, the toughest prison in America, as a cinematic statement of his importance in the criminal world.

THE FIRST CINEMATIC ESCAPE OFF ALCATRAZ
House Across the Bay is the first movie to actually show someone escaping off the island. This is also the most outrageously false Alcatraz aspect of the film. Not only does Larwitt escape, he does it on the spur of the moment, without planning. He hops a wall, jumps into the water, swims to San Francisco, runs into a dark road, fakes being hurt, beats up a man, steals his car, drives to the east side of the bay, and then a few hours later, does it all again, in the reverse direction. (In between swims, he also tries to strangle his wife and then murders his lawyer.) Now that's one tough guy. Still, at the end, one of the characters observes, "What a sucker the guy is to try to escape from Alcatraz. Nobody ever made it."

"Just another Jenny with a Johnny on the Rock"

Mary Bogel, Alcatraz rock widow, *House Across the Bay*
Reference to the women whose men are incarcerated on Alcatraz

"I can't go on without you baby. It's like taking the breath out of my body. I just can't do it."

Steve Larwitt to Brenda Bentley upon being sentenced to ten years on Alcatraz, *House Across the Bay*

STARRING

A GANGSTER'S GANGSTER

GEORGE RAFT (Steve Larwitt) built his seven-decade-long film career starring as a tough mob boss in many of Hollywood's top gangster films. Raft was born in the Hell's Kitchen area of New York City and was boyhood friends with real-life gangsters Ben "Bugsy" Siegel and Owney Madden. His association with these men put into question Raft's own role in the criminal world, a reputation that played well with the public, especially in his early films. Raft worked with top directors and stars: Howard Hawks in *Scarface* (1932); Raoul Walsh in *They Drive by Night* (1940); and, parodying his own image, in Billy Wilder's great gangster comedy, *Some Like it Hot* (1959). Raft is well cast in *House Across the Bay*, giving his characteristic tough-guy performance, but Bennett's spunk brings out the best in his soft side as well. His last words are delivered with his signature spark: "Bye, baby. You're still tops with me." In Raft's later years, he again parodied his screen persona in another Alcatraz-connected film, *Skidoo* (1968).

JOAN BENNETT (Brenda Bentley) starred in many Hollywood films of the '40s and '50s, including *Woman in the Window* (1944), *Scarlet Street* (1945), and *Father of the Bride* (1950). Known for her beauty, Bennett, who gives an assured, brash performance as the woman who intoxicates Raft, is showcased in two highly effective musical numbers; though her voice is small, she sings her own songs. The first, *"Walking my Chihuahua,"* is fun and provocative, performed in full Carmen Miranda attire: turban of fruit, floral skirt, and midriff-bearing top. The second, *"I Know I'll Be a Fool Again,"* is a melodramatic lament (beautifully lit by Merritt B. Gerstad) about falling in love with the wrong man. Bennett came from a theatrical family; both her father and mother were in the theater, and her sister was noted film actress Constance Bennett.

LLOYD NOLAN (Slant Kolma) was often cast as the bad guy in his early film career. Raft's character, Steve Larwitt, is the mob boss, but Nolan's shady, jealous lawyer Kolma is the true villain. Nolan's acting career started in the 1935 classic gangster film, *G-Men*, starring James Cagney, and went on to include over one hundred films, from gangster to Westerns, melodramas, and comedies. Nolan joined Paramount in 1937 in the first *Dr. Kildare* film, *Interns Can't Take Money*. At 20th Century Fox, he starred in a series of popular B-list movies as the crime-fighting Irish American detective Michael McShayne. His films include *Wells Fargo* (1937), *Bataan* (1943), *A Tree Grows in Brooklyn* (1945), *Peyton Place* (1957), and *Airport* (1970). *House* was not Nolan's only film with an Alcatraz connection; he had starred with Robert Preston two years earlier in *King of Alcatraz*.

WALTER PIDGEON (Tim Nolan) was about to become one of Hollywood's leading men in 1940 when *House Across the Bay* was released. Tall and handsome, Pidgeon's role as a rich, sophisticated airplane designer in *House* suited him well, but it wasn't until the following year that his career took off with the leading role in the award-winning *How Green Was My Valley* (1941). He followed it with many first-rate films, including Oscar-nominated performances in *Mrs. Miniver* (1942) and *Madame Curie* (1943). His films include *Julia Misbehaves* (1948), *The Bad and the Beautiful* (1952), *Executive Suite* (1954), *Forbidden Planet* (1956), and *Advise and Consent* (1962). A year after *House*, Pidgeon and Bennett stared together in Fritz Lang's thriller, *Man Hunt*. Pidgeon's last film was the '70s bomb *Sextette* (1978), starring Mae West, in which he and George Raft had small parts (Raft played himself).

GLADYS GEORGE (Mary Bogel) was a gifted comedian, but often cast in dramatic roles, winning an Oscar nomination in 1936 for *Valiant Is a Name for Carrie*. George brings her comedic skills to *House Across the Bay* and steals most of her scenes as a tough, sweet prison wife who befriends Bennett. George was splendid in the tearjerker, *Madame X* (1937), and became a great character actress, appearing in *Marie Antoinette* (1938), *The Best Years of Our Lives* (1946), and *Detective Story* (1951), but she is often remembered as Iva Archer, the widow of Sam Spade's partner in the film noir classic, *The Maltese Falcon* (1941).

VISITORS' ROOM, CIRCA 1950

BEHIND THE SCENES

Director ARCHIE MAYO created an engaging prison romance in *House Across the Bay*, keeping the action fast-paced, and bringing out the best in his two leads. Mayo worked with top Hollywood stars and craftsmen in the '20s, '30s, and '40s. As a contract director at Warner Brothers from 1927 to 1937, adept at drama, action, musicals, and comedies, he was at the helm of over forty films made in a ten-year period. Notable are *Svengali* (1931) with John Barrymore at his most "entrancing"; *Go Into Your Dance* (1935), an Al Jolson musical; the crime drama *The Petrified Forest* (1936); and *Black Legion* (1937), a powerful social drama with Bogart in his first leading role. In 1930, Mayo directed *The Doorway to Hell*. It's significant for introducing the "Tommy-gun in the violin case" to the gangster genre. At Paramount, Mayo directed Raft in his first starring role, *Night After Night* (1932). The film also introduced Mae West, who stole the picture and became a star as a result. In his later years, Mayo developed a reputation as being a difficult director. His last films included the popular *Charley's Aunt* (1941), *Orchestra Wives* (1942), *Crash Dive* (1943), and *A Night in Casablanca* and *Angel on My Shoulder* (both 1946).

Producer WALTER WANGER (born Walter Feuchtwanger in San Francisco, California) was behind some of the Hollywood's most lavish and admired films, including *Queen Christina* (1933) with Greta Garbo; *Joan of Arc* (1948) with Ingrid Bergman; and the most expensive motion picture in its day, the 1963 version of *Cleopatra* with Elizabeth Taylor. Wanger began his own production company, Walter Wanger Productions, and in addition to *House Across the Bay*, produced *Algiers* (1938), *Stagecoach* (1939), *Foreign Correspondent* (1940), *Scarlet Street* (1945), the original version of *Invasion of the Body Snatchers* (1956, directed by Don Siegel, *Escape from Alcatraz*), and the prison drama *I Want to Live* (1958). At Paramount, Wanger worked with many notable directors and produced films with all three *House* leads. George Raft in *Every Night at Eight* (1935), directed by Raoul Walsh; Walter Pidgeon in *Fatal Lady* (1936), directed by Edward Ludwig; and Joan Bennett in two films, *Private World* (1935), directed by Gregory La Cava, and Walsh's *Big Brown Eyes* (1936), with Cary Grant.

HOLLYWOOD CONFIDENTIAL

Producer Wanger's personal life was one of Hollywood's biggest stories, with odd echoes of *House Across the Bay*. In 1951 Wanger discovered his actress wife (of ten years) having an affair with her agent, Jennings Lang, and shot the man in the groin (he fully recovered). His wife was none other than *House Across the Bay* star, Joan Bennett. Remarkably, their marriage lasted another fourteen years. Wanger served two years in prison, and upon his release produced *Riot in Cell Block 11* (1954), directed by Don Siegel. The picture was a seminal film in the history of prison dramas, commenting on poor conditions in prisons with understanding and balance (no doubt acquired from his personal experience behind bars), a topic rarely discussed in the '50s.

Original Story Writer MYLES CONNOLLY was a former newspaper reporter who began his Hollywood career at the fledgling RKO studio, where he befriended the young Frank Capra. He moved to MGM, writing entertaining films, including two Tarzan features and the musical *Music for Millions* (1944 Oscar nomination). He worked with Capra on *State of the Union* (1948) and *Here Comes the Groom* (1952). His last screenplay was the musical *Hans Christian Andersen* (1952).

Screenwriter KATHRYN SCOLA's sharp script portrays the tough world of gangsters, but maintains a breezy '40s style. Her snappy dialogue for the Alcatraz "Rock widows" is catty and funny, referring to newcomer Bennett as "just another Jenny with a Johnny on the Rock." In 1930, Kathryn Scola began her Hollywood career writing *One Night at Susie's* (with Forrest Halsey), starring Billie Dove and Douglas Fairbanks Jr. Scola wrote comedies, dramas, musicals, mysteries, and adventure films. Many of her early films starred complex female characters portrayed by stars Loretta Young and Barbara Stanwyck, for whom she worked on the notorious film *Baby Face* (1932). In 1936, Scola went to the new 20th Century Fox Studio, where her films included *The Constant Nymph* (1943), *Alexander's Ragtime Band* (1938), and *Submarine Patrol* (1938). Scola's last screenplay was the 1949 *Night Unto Night*, directed by Don Siegel and starring Ronald Reagan.

Cinematographer MERRITT B. GERSTAD beautifully photographs *House Across the Bay*. In one exceptional moment toward the end of the film, Raft, who has just broken out of prison, waits outside a nightclub to see if Bennett will join him. It's a foggy night and the screen is white, when suddenly, Bennett breaks though the haze, appearing out of nowhere, as in a dream. Gerstad shot many popular Hollywood films, including *Imitation of Life* (1934), *Night at the Opera* (1935), and *Watch on the Rhine* (1943).

Editor DOROTHY SPENCER started working at 20th Century Fox in 1929, the year the studio began, when she was twenty years old. Her first film was a musical, *Married in Hollywood* (1929). She won her first Oscar nomination in 1939 for John Ford's classic western, *Stagecoach*. Spencer worked on comedies, dramas, westerns, action pictures, and epics, receiving three more Oscar nominations. Spencer's career spanned seventy films over sixty years. Her remarkable filmography is a "who's who" of movies and directors. They include *Foreign Correspondent* (1940, Alfred Hitchcock), *Heaven Can Wait* (1943, Ernest Lubitsch), *A Tree Grows in Brooklyn* (1945, Elia Kazan), *Black Widow*, (1954, Nunnally Johnson), *A Hatful of Rain* (1957, Fred Zinnemann), *The Young Lions* (1958, Edward Dmytryk), and *Cleopatra* (1963, Joseph L. Mankiewicz).

Set Decorator JULIA HERON was at the top of her field when she made *House Across the Bay*. Heron received four Oscar nominations, winning in 1960 for the epic *Spartacus*. Her films include *The Westerner* (1940), *The Woman in the Window* (1945, starring Joan Bennett), *The Best Years of Our Lives* (1946), and *Written on the Wind* (1956).

Composers **IRVING ACTMAN**, **GEORGE R. BROWN**, **SIDNEY CLARE**, **WERNER JANSSEN**, **AL SIEGEL**, and the celebrated **JULE STYNE** created a moving score for *House* and a particularly tender melody as the love theme for Raft and Bennett that plays throughout the movie. The two musical numbers are fun, poignant, and very entertaining. Of the group, Jule Styne became the most well known, creating hit musicals, many of which were turned into films, including *Peter Pan* (1954), *Bells Are Ringing* (1956), *Gypsy* (1959), and *Funny Girl* (1964).

Lyricist **NICK CASTLE** not only composed music and wrote lyrics, he was a famous film choreographer. A vaudeville performer before joining 20th Century Fox in 1937, he worked at many of the major studios and with leading stars, including Shirley Temple, Gene Kelly, and Fred Astaire. There is no choreography credit on *House Across the Bay*, but Castle may very well have staged Bennett's musical numbers. His lyrics for Bennett's two songs in *House* are provocatively charming in *"Walking My Chihuahua,"* and resigned to misery in *"I Know I'll Be a Fool Again."*

film poster

In the Spanish version poster for *House Across the Bay*, the title was changed to *El Gangster y la Bailarina*, implying a more illicit romance, playing off Raft's dangerous reputation and Bennett's sophistication. This more romantic title is appropriate to the film's central love story, and more marketable as a tough romance than a tough prison drama. In 1940, Alcatraz was not as well known internationally and its location as "a house across a bay," would not have had any relevance for Europeans. The slang use of the word "house" for prison also may not have translated to an audience in Spain. However, Hollywood film stars Raft and Bennett themselves translated well.

SAN FRANCISCO DOCKS

Directed by
ARTHUR LUBIN

UNIVERSAL PICTURES
66 minutes, black and white

CAST

Burgess Meredith	Johnny Barnes
Irene Hervey	Kitty Tracy
Raymond Walburn	Admiral Andy Tracy
Barry Fitzgerald	Icky
Robert Armstrong	Father Cameron
Lewis Howard	Sanford
Edward Gargan	Hank
Esther Ralston	Frances March
Edward Pawley	Monte March
Don Zelaya	Felipe
Joe Downing	Cassidy

CREATIVE

Producer	Marshall Grant
Story	Martin Mooney
Screenplay	Edmund L. Hartmann, Stanley Rubin
Cinematography	Charles Van Enger
Editing	Bernard W. Burton
Art Direction	Harold H. MacArthur
	Jack Otterson
Set Decoration	Russell A. Gausman
Original Music	Hans J. Salter, Charles Previn
	Frank Skinner
Costumes (gowns)	Vera West

THE STORY

One night, a riot erupts at the notorious prison on Alcatraz Island. Four men clamber over the enormous walls that surround the prison attempting to escape. Searchlights spot them, shots are fired, and two men are killed. The other two jump into the water, but when they swim out into the bay, one of the convicts, big-time gangster Monte Marsh, quickly drowns the other, and then heads toward the sound of Spanish music and a waiting boat. The police search the bay, but can't find the men and assume the tides swept them out to sea.

That same night, longshoreman Johnny Barnes goes to a wharf bar, where his girlfriend Kitty works. Johnny finds City Attorney Bill Cassidy flirting with Kitty, and the two men start throwing punches. Cassidy is tossed out, and after quarrelling with Kitty, Johnny leaves and roams the foggy San Francisco docks. Alcatraz escapee Monte Marsh has reached the shore, and has been lurking around the docks too. When he sees Cassidy—the man who put him in Alcatraz—leave the bar, he follows him.

Later that night, Cassidy is found dead, and suspicion falls on Johnny who, with no alibi, gets thrown in jail. All Johnny can remember is hearing Spanish music as he wandered around the dock area.

Kitty knows Johnny is innocent and gets her father, Johnny's friend Hank, Father Cameron, and town barfly Icky to search the dock for clues. In jail, Johnny overhears another prisoner, Felipe, singing in Spanish. He gets a message to Kitty, who bails Felipe out and tricks him into revealing that Marsh didn't drown when he escaped from Alcatraz, but was plucked out of the bay and taken by boat to the docks.

Marsh has been hiding out with his wife Frances, but when he hears that Johnny's been convicted of Cassidy's murder, he feels it's safe to leave. He arranges with trawler owner Bill Collins to take a boat to South America, but Icky and Hank overhear Collins tell his crew the plan. Kitty has an idea. She finds a picture of Mrs. Marsh in the newspaper and sees that Frances is quite a blond bombshell. She scours beauty shops in the area and finds out where Frances gets her hair done. Then she sets a trap, figuring that someone like Frances will go to the beauty parlor before she leaves the country. Kitty's hunch pays off when Frances shows up. The gang is ready when Frances leaves, and they follow her home and find Marsh. Marsh climbs out the window, but Kitty makes sure Frances doesn't go anywhere. The gang gets help from all the longshoremen as they chase Marsh through the city. Father Cameron, an old high school pal of Marsh's who took a different path in life, pins him down. Everyone at the bar celebrates Johnny's release, especially Kitty.

S.F. WATERFRONT, 1940S, LONGSHOREMEN LOADING CARGO

THE INSIDE SCOOP

The majority of Universal's releases into the '50s were predictable B pictures. The studio's output was impressive, releasing hundreds of these entertaining, if undistinguished, films. *San Francisco Docks* was made with Universal's contract talent, but as directed by Arthur Lubin, it is above the standard fare, with a lively screenplay, effective score, and a memorable cast. Walburn, acting in his signature blowhard style and Fitzgerald, in his over-the-top Irish manner, spar throughout the film, adding considerable fun to the proceedings. Though Burgess Meredith is the lead, and there's lots of testosterone on display, it's sensible and strong Irene Hervey who outsmarts the police, her bumbling crew, and the gangsters to save the day. Her beauty parlor sleuthing is a particularly fun plot device. San Francisco's foggy shoreline is handsomely realized in the mysterious nighttime scenes, and setting the film along the city's famous Barbary Coast with its rich and steamy history adds a vivid context to the storyline. Like most good B movies, Lubin keeps the action moving, the comedy swift, and the lovers apart until the last reel.

ALCATRAZ: REEL TO REAL

An Alcatraz prison escape early in the film is the catalyst for the action, and it's a swift and rousing sequence. It has all the right elements: a nighttime breakout, a thrilling score, fast editing, shadowy lighting, and a dive into murky water surrounding the island. As portrayed in *San Francisco Docks*, Alcatraz was an easy prison from which to escape, (this pattern of easy escapes in most of the early Alcatraz movies was so prevalent that it's a wonder they managed to keep anyone locked up at all). In fact, Alcatraz was billed as an escape-proof prison, and the Bureau of Prisons did everything it could to make sure the prison lived up to its reputation. However, by 1940, there had been four escape attempts, including one by Ralph Roe and Theodore Cole, who were never found.

The escape scene shows prisoners walking along the top of a cement wall, when, in fact, there is no cement wall around Alcatraz Island. Rather than building walls, the Bureau of Prisons encircled the prison areas of the island with cyclone fencing and coils of barbed wire. The only walled area is a concrete "stockade" enclosure surrounding the convicts' exercise yard.

the studio: UNIVERSAL

Founded in 1912 by Carl Laemmle, Universal Studios had early success in the silent-film era. The studio flourished in 1915, when Laemmle consolidated his small East- and West Coast production facilities and purchased 230 acres in California, which he named Universal City. Laemmle's business strategy was to produce a large number of low-budget films, with an emphasis on quantity.

Universal explored the horror and fantasy genres, with an early version of Jules Verne's *20,000 Leagues Under the Sea* (1916), and *Phantom of the Opera* (1925). In 1931, it solidified its "horror" standing with the release of *Dracula* (starring Bela Lugosi) and *Frankenstein* (starring Boris Karloff).

Universal's films, included melodramas (*Magnificent Obsession*, 1935), Deanna Durbin musicals, romantic comedies (*My Man Godfrey*, 1936), Sherlock Holmes mysteries, *Abbott and Costello* features, and *Arabian Night* adventures. By the late '40s, Universal dropped serials, cut back on musicals, and began to produce more high-quality films, including *The Naked City* (1948), *Winchester '73* (1950), *Touch of Evil* (1958), *Pillow Talk* (1959), and *Spartacus* (1960). By the '80s and '90s, they were back in the fantasy business with *E.T. the Extra-Terrestrial* (1982), *Back to the Future* (1985), and *Jurassic Park* (1993).

STARRING

BURGESS MEREDITH (Johnny) received acclaim for one of his first roles, playing George in John Steinbeck's *Of Mice and Men* (1939) directed by Lewis Milestone. He made two poplar romantic comedies in 1941, *Tom, Dick and Harry*, directed by Garson Kanin, and *That Uncertain Feeling*, directed by Ernest Lubtisch. After serving in the air force in WWII, Meredith starred in William Wellman's Story of *GI Joe* (1945). Meredith's career came to a sudden halt in the early '50s when he was named an unfriendly witness by the House Un-American Activities Committee, and his career didn't pick up again until the 1960s after the McCarthy witch-hunts ended. Once back on-screen, the actor appeared in over ninety films and television shows over the next thirty-four years. Meredith worked with Otto Preminger on *Advise and Consent* (1962), *The Cardinal* (1963), *In Harm's Way* (1965), *Hurry Sundown* (1967), *Skidoo* (1968—Burgess appeared as Alcatraz's warden), and *Such Good Friends* (1971). At age 68, Meredith received his first Oscar nomination for *The Day of the Locust* (1975), followed with another nomination for his role as Sylvester Stallone's trainer Mickey, in *Rocky* (1976). In 1995, at the age of 84, Meredith made his final film, the Howard Deutch comedy, *Grumpier Old Men*.

IRENE HERVEY (Kitty Tracy) takes charge in *San Francisco Docks*, leading a group of bungling men. At 24, Hervey made her first film, *The Stranger's Return* (1933), directed by King Vidor. She continued in supporting and lead roles throughout the '30s and '40s. In the '50s, Hervey started a successful television career that including a recurring role as Aunt Meg in *Honey West* (1965–66). Hervey's last feature film was *Play Misty for Me* (1971), Clint Eastwood's directorial debut.

BARRY FITZGERALD (Icky) makes the most of every line and every on-screen moment. His malleable face and familiar Irish character graced many films, including *Bringing Up Baby* (1938), *How Green Was My Valley* (1941), *None But the Lonely Heart* (1944), and *The Quiet Man* (1952). Fitzgerald, who played against type in the hit Universal crime drama, *Naked City* (1948), is remembered for his 1944 Oscar-winning performance as Father Fitzgibbon in *Going My Way*.

RAYMOND WALBURN (Admiral Andy Tracy) brought his trademark blowhard character to *San Francisco Docks*. Walburn started his career in silent films and easily transitioned to talkies, in notable films including Preston Sturgess's *Hail the Conquering Hero* (1944) and Frank Capra's *Mr. Deeds Goes to Town* (1936). Walburn starred in Monogram Picture's *"Father"* series as boastful patriarch Henry Latham.

ROBERT ARMSTRONG (Father Cameron) battled *King Kong* (1933) before he fought gangster Monte Marsh in *San Francisco Docks*. His gangster films included *The Cop* (1928), *"G" Men* (1935), and *Public Enemy's Wife* (1936). Armstrong's role as the adventurous Carl Denham in the classic *King Kong* and its sequel, *The Son of Kong*, assured him a place in movie history.

"Hey, who they chasing?"

"I don't know, but they're longshoremen, let's go."

San Francisco Docks

BEHIND THE SCENES

Director ARTHUR LUBIN joined Universal Studios in 1936, where he worked for ten years, and subsequently returned to Universal in 1949 and stayed for another eight years. Lubin primarily directed enjoyable lightweight movies, and was behind some of Abbott and Costello's best and most successful films, including *Buck Private*, *In the Navy*, and *Hold That Ghost* (all 1941). His skill in filming the famous duo was all the more admirable given that Costello was notorious for his wild antics on the set (many hilarious moments have been included in these films, but he was often prone to off-color remarks which were left on the cutting room floor). Lubin's success with Abbott and Costello is said to have saved Universal from bankruptcy. His gift at directing comedy (especially teams) is clearly evident in *San Francisco Docks* where he gives ample screen time to the delightful banter between Walburn and Fitzgerald. At Universal, as did many of their talent, Lubin worked in many genres, from horror films (*Black Friday*, 1940), gangster films, comedies, Westerns, and mysteries, to campy fantasies like *Ali-Baba and the 40 Thieves* (1944) and *The Spider Woman Strikes Back* (1946). Lubin's most financially successful film was the 1943 version of *Phantom of the Opera*, starring Claude Rains. Lubin directed a popular film series starring Roddy McDowell and "Francis," a talking mule. He later recreated that success with the television series *Mr. Ed* (1961). Lubin moved to the small screen as second-reelers waned, directing the Westerns *Maverick* and *Bronco* (1958), *Bonanza* (1959), and the stylish detective series *77 Sunset Strip* (1958).

Editor BERNARD W. BURTON was part of Universal's company of talent, editing in every genre including horror, comedy, crime, drama, and musicals. Among his many films are *Show Boat* and *The Invisible Ray* (both 1936), *The Rage of Paris* (1938), and Deanna Durbin's best films, *One Hundred Men and a Girl* (1937), *That Certain Age* (1938), and *It Started with Eve* (1941). Burton was also a producer and was behind a comedy/drama series for Monogram Pictures Corporation based on Ham Fisher's comic book character "Joe Palooka".

Screenwriter MARTIN MOONEY was known for his many prison and crime stories. His notable films include *Special Agent* (1935), with Bette Davis, his first picture; the tough cop story, *Bullets or Ballots* (1936), with Edward G. Robinson; and the crime drama, *Crime, Inc.* (1945). Mooney's writing was well informed by his years as a New York City newspaper reporter and columnist. He served as producer and associate producer on over twenty films, including Columbia Studio's Alcatraz film, *Devil Ship* (1947).

Screenwriters EDWARD L. HARTMANN and **STANLEY RUBIN** brought their comedic flair to *San Francisco Docks*. Rubin wrote screenplays for Abbott and Costello and Martin and Lewis films. Hartmann was a top comedy writer and had a long and successful collaboration with Bob Hope, writing many of his funniest films, including *Sorrowful Jones* (1949), *Fancy Pants* (1950), and *My Favorite Spy* (1951).

BARBER SHOP, NORTH END OF "A" BLOCK

Cinematographer CHARLES VAN ENGER began his career in the silent-film era, working on dozens of films, including King Vidor's epic *The Big Parade* (1925). Van Enger joined Universal in 1936, and for fourteen years was part of their stable of talent, creating movies in every genre including *"Sherlock Holmes"* mysteries, musicals, and Westerns. His work on *San Francisco Docks* is particularly evocative, especially the early scenes along the foggy nighttime Barbary Coast.

Set Decorator RUSSELL A. GAUSMAN won six Oscar nominations and two statues for art direction and set direction—one for the Arthur Lubin film *Phantom of the Opera* (1943), and one in 1961 for *Spartacus*. Gausman worked at Universal for thirty-five years on more than six hundred films, reflecting the incredible history of Universal Studios. Gausman's first film was the 1925 silent classic *Phantom of the Opera*, followed by *Dracula* in 1931. His many celebrated films include *Arabian Nights* (1942), *The Killers* (1946), *Man Without a Star* (1955), *The Incredible Shrinking Man* (1957), and *Touch of Evil* (1958).

Composers HANS J. SLATER, **CHARLES PREVIN**, and **FRANK SKINNER** all worked for many years at Universal Studios. Together and separately, they created music that can be heard in literally hundreds of films in every genre. Between them, they received a dozen Oscar nominations, many for singing sensation Deanna Durbin, whose popular films were fundamental to Universal's financial health in the '40s.

film poster

Universal Studio's first advertising manager was Robert Cochrane, who hired his brother Phillip and Karoly Grosz as art directors. They created some of the studio's most dynamic posters—including *Phantom of the Opera* (1925), and *Dracula* and *Frankenstein* (both 1931)—which are especially sought-after by collectors. When Cochrane left in 1937, the studio's poster quality suffered, and it wasn't until 1942, when Maurice Kallis was brought in from Paramount, that their quality was resurrected.

The poster for *San Francisco Docks* is from its 1950 re-release, which may be behind its disjointed combination of themes and styles. The upper portion of the poster is a watercolor showing an action-packed fight scene along the docks, but the costumes have a fictitious French flair, complete with berets, though the story is American gangsters and longshoremen through and through. The frightened female at the top wearing a short red dress has no connection to Irene Hervey's feisty Kitty, a blue-collar worker. Photographic images show Barry Fitzgerald looking mean and Walburn forceful, contradicting their jester roles. While individual elements of the poster are interesting—the photos are amusing; the watercolors, handsome; and the titles, striking—it appears to have been assembled from a variety of sources. Regardless of its uneven quality, it is an exciting visual from the golden age of film, with a great typeface for the title.

Produced by Realart, this is a typical "one-sheet" (27" x 41"), which was considered a standard element of printed movie poster advertising. Realart produced all of Universal's re-releases from the late '40s to the early '50s (the film was originally released in 1941). On the bottom right corner below the image is the code R50/665. "R" indicates re-issue; "50," the year 1950; and "665" denotes that this was the 665th movie poster Realart had produced that year.

SEVEN MILES FROM ALCATRAZ

Directed by
EDWARD DMYTRYK

RKO PICTURES
62 minutes, black and white

CAST

James Craig	Champ Larkin
Bonita Granville	Anne Porter
Frank Jenks	Jimbo
Cliff Edwards	Stormy
George Cleveland	Captain Porter
Erford Gage	Paul Brenner
Tala Birell	Baroness
John Banner	Fritz Weinermann
Otto Reichow	Max

CREATIVE

Producer	Herman Schlom
Story	John D. Klorer
Screenplay	Joseph Krumgold
Cinematography	Robert De Grasse
Editing	George Crone
Original Music	Roy Web

SEVEN MILES
FROM
ALCATRAZ
with JAMES CRAIG
BONITA GRANVILLE
and FRANK JENKS · CLIFF EDWARDS
RKO
RADIO
PICTURES
Produced by
HERMAN SCHLOM
Directed by
EDWARD DMYTRYK
SCREEN PLAY BY JOSEPH KRUMGOLD
Copyright 1942 RKO Radio Pictures Inc. Country of Origin U. S. A.
MORGAN LITHO. CORP. CLEVELAND, O.
PROPERTY OF NATIONAL SCREEN SERVICE CORP. LICENSED FOR DISPLAY ONLY IN CONNECTION WITH THE EXHIBITION OF THIS PICTURE AT YOUR THEATRE. MUST BE RETURNED IMMEDIATELY THEREAFTER.
42/550
23511.

THE STORY

During WWII, Alcatraz cellmates Champ Larkin and Jimbo are happy to find out that prisoners can't be sent to the battlefield, but as the war goes on, even the federal penitentiary at Alcatraz is affected. There's no wood in the carpentry shop, no metal in the metal shop, and no thread in the sewing shop. All prisoners can do is listen to planes flying overhead.

Trapped on Alcatraz, Champ and Jimbo, feeling like sitting targets, plan an escape. In the dead of night, they jump into the bay, just miss being shot, and are carried by the tide under the Golden Gate Bridge. They sight a lighthouse on a tiny island and head toward it. Climbing ashore, they quickly overwhelm the lighthouse keeper, Captain Porter, his daughter Anne, and two assistants, Stormy and Paul Brenner. They hold the group hostage as they plan their next move. Champ takes a quick liking to Anne, and though she is attracted to the tall and handsome Champ, his actions and disinterest in the war effort disgust her.

Unbeknownst to the others, Brenner secretly takes a message off the Morse code machine, and sends it via radio to a German submarine heading to blow up San Francisco. Brenner then sends the same message to his Nazi compatriots in San Francisco, who must transfer crucial plans from Brenner to the submarine. Suddenly, over the radio comes the call for a blackout. Champ and Jimbo, fearing they'll be caught, rush to the lighthouse's small boat to get away, the same boat Brenner wants to deliver the plans to his Nazi gang. A fight ensues and Champ overpowers Brenner, gets his gun, and kills him. Just then, the blackout is called off and Champ and Jimbo return to the lighthouse. When Brenner doesn't appear with the plans, his Nazi associates show up at the lighthouse and another big fight breaks out. All seems lost, until Champ and Jimbo overtake the spies, foil the Nazis' plans, and become reluctant heroes. US forces are alerted and bomb the sub into oblivion. For their bravery, Champ and Jimbo are released from Alcatraz.

CARGO NETS, MADE BY INMATES FOR MILITARY USE DURING WWII

PRISON, AERIAL VIEW FROM EAST

THE INSIDE SCOOP

Seven Miles from Alcatraz appeared in theaters on November 10, 1942, not quite a year after America entered WWII. Hollywood became an important part of the war effort, producing propaganda films that supported the nation at home and overseas. *Seven Miles* is a unique entry in this category, with two unlikely Alcatraz prisoners saving San Francisco from annihilation. "We may be hoodlums, but we're American hoodlums," declares Champ Larkin after defeating the Nazi spies. With an energetic score from Roy Webb and effective cinematography from Robert De Grasse, director Edward Dmytryk crafts a tight, fast-paced action movie. The story is overt in its war sentiment, and lacks any real tension, but remains an entertaining second feature, promoting an important anti-Nazi message to all Americans, even criminals.

The movie opens with the customary slightly rocking view of Alcatraz Island filmed from a boat—in 1942, filmmakers could not get close to the working prison. A shaky aerial shot affords viewers an interesting perspective of the island's architectural layout, but after that, it's pure Hollywood, showing enormous factories with guards patrolling the catwalks; large prison cells with bunk beds; and an outdoor recreation yard the size of two football fields. The prisoners are relaxed, easy-going, nice guys, leaving us to wonder why they'd be locked up in a maximum-security penitentiary in the first place. Equally confounding, but not atypical, is the ease with which they escape. In a jovial voiceover, hero Champ Larkin declines to reveal their method, due to "professional secrecy." The Nazi spies dress in furs and tuxedos, smoke cigarettes, and have cocktails in a swanky San Francisco apartment. Their extravagant lifestyle is portrayed as amoral, particularly when juxtaposed against the modest lighthouse staff doing its best to protect America.

the studio: **RKO**

RKO Studios came into existence in 1929 as a result of a series of mergers that took place when "talkies" were becoming popular. Chairman David Sarnoff, who was committed to making prestigious films, began with a Ziegfeld musical extravaganza, *Rio Rita* (1929). RKO's history is one of ever-changing management, which hindered it from establishing the consistent artistic (and financial) footing of other major studios. As a result, RKO created great films in every genre, depending on who was in charge. Among its many memorable movies were spectacular adventures like *King Kong* and *Gunga Din* (both 1939), Astaire–Rogers musicals, Katherine Hepburn and Cary Grant comedies, Hitchcock mysteries, and film noir classics. *Seven Miles from Alcatraz* was one of many low-budget films that RKO released throughout the '40s. The studio created its own unique style, producing hundreds of films and maintaining a strong momentum until its demise in the 1950s under the erratic leadership of Howard Hughes. RKO is credited with creating the film noir look when it released Orson Wells' *Citizen Kane* (1940), filmed by cinematographer Greg Toland. *Seven Miles* director Edward Dmytryk became a key figure in the noir style with his acclaimed 1944 film, *Murder, My Sweet.*

WWII ANTI-AIRCRAFT GUN WITH CREW ON ALCATRAZ ROOF   WWII NET BUOYS

"This is your war, whether you like it or not. It's being fought all over the world, by every storekeeper, preacher, ditch-digger, and even gangster."

Lighthouse captain Porter to escaped Alcatraz prisoner Champ Larkin, *Seven Miles from Alcatraz*

ALCATRAZ: REEL TO REAL

In fact, there is no island with a lighthouse located seven miles from Alcatraz; the nearest islands with lights are East Brother Light off Point Richmond (about ten miles from Alcatraz and about one mile from the Golden Gate Bridge) and Mile Rock Light near San Francisco's Lands End (five miles away).

The industries on Alcatraz are shown as dwindling to nothing from lack of supplies as a result of the war effort, but in reality, James A. Johnston, the prison's first warden, increased Alcatraz's industries to aid the war effort. The tailor shop shifted from making prison uniforms to making military uniforms for the army and Marine Corps. To fulfill the navy's need for oversized cargo nets, a net shop was set up; it was so successful that the navy commended Alcatraz on its efforts.

As the film opens, Champ and Jimbo read about the attack on Pearl Harbor in a newspaper in their cell. In fact, prisoners' only official source of war news came from the edited dispatches shared with them by the warden. During the prison's early years, inmates had no access to magazines and newspapers, which was intended to isolate them from the outside world. On December 7, 1941, the news about the attack on Pearl Harbor was written on a chalkboard at the entrance to the dining hall, and was read by prisoners as they came in from their Sunday baseball game in the Recreation Yard.

Champ and Jimbo are shown sharing a cell, when in fact, Alcatraz inmates were housed one to a cell. The film shows an aerial view of the island as Champ tells us that there are 800 prisoners on Alcatraz. Even at its height, USP Alcatraz housed a maximum of only 302 inmates at any one time.

As in many early Alcatraz films, Champ and Jimbo easily escape the island by jumping into San Francisco Bay and swimming away. In fact, there were three escape attempts during WWII, though none of the convicts succeeded. *(See pages 95 and 115 for the real stories.)*

"We may be hoodlums, but we're American hoodlums."

Champ Larkin, *Seven Miles From Alcatraz*

STARRING

JAMES CRAIG's (Champ) good looks made him a minor matinee idol in twenty-two Hollywood films, from Westerns and war dramas to breezy comedies. The easy-going Craig started his career at age 25 as a contract player for Paramount. When Craig signed with RKO Pictures, he landed more significant roles. Notable as Ginger Rogers' love interest in *Kitty Foyle* (1940), and as the deal-making New England farmer in *The Devil and Daniel Webster* (1941), Craig made his last appearance for RKO in *Seven Miles from Alcatraz*. When Craig joined MGM, he received consistent second leads (and occasionally was top-billed) with stars including Lana Turner, Marlene Dietrich, and Mickey Rooney.

BONITA GRANVILLE (Anne) had a very active film career in the '30s and '40s. At 13, she received an Oscar nomination as Best Supporting Actress for her portrayal of a vicious child gossip in *These Three* (1936), an adaptation by Lillian Hellman of her play, *The Children's Hour*. Granville had secondary parts in major films, including *The Mortal Storm* (1940) and *Now Voyager* (1942), but is remembered as Nancy Drew in the popular mystery/detective series based on the classic chapter books. Granville's adult career never matched her youthful screen roles, and she left acting in the early '50s. She went on to become a producer and director of the popular television show *Lassie*.

FRANK JENKS (Jimbo) was a character actor who made more than one hundred Hollywood films, playing a bartender, truck driver, piano mover, mailman, or cab driver. Jenks worked for major studios in mysteries, Westerns, musicals, and comedies, including *His Girl Friday* (1940) and *Christmas in Connecticut* (1945). In 1950, Jenks began a string of television appearances, including *The Adventures of Superman* (1952) and *Perry Mason* (1957).

CLIFF EDWARDS' (Stormy) name and face may not be familiar to many, but his voice is known to millions of children and adults as Pinocchio's conscience, Jiminy Cricket, in Disney's 1940 animated film (as Jiminy, he performed the Oscar-winning song, *When You Wish Upon a Star*). Edwards also provided the voice of Jim Crow in *Dumbo* (1941), singing *When I See an Elephant Fly*. Edwards was a famous ukulele player (inducted into the Ukulele Hall of Fame Museum in 2000) and brought this talent to many B Westerns as Harmony Haines, Harmony Stubbs, Harmony Bumpas, and Cliff *"Ukulele Ike"* Edwards.

JOHN BANNER (Fritz Weinermann) came to America in the early '40s from Germany, during WWII. He made nearly fifty movies, but had his greatest success in television, where he appeared in over seventy-five shows between the 1950s and the 1970s. He is most often remembered as the German Sergeant Schultz in the hit television series *Hogan's Heroes* (1965 to 1971). Ironically, Banner, who was Jewish, had spent time as a prisoner in a Nazi concentration camp.

BEHIND THE SCENES

Director EDWARD DMYTRYK was born in Canada and grew up in San Francisco. He directed B pictures at both Paramount and Columbia studios before arriving at RKO. The studio was known for hiring young, gifted directors, the list of whom included George Cukor, John Ford, George Stevens, Howard Hawks, and Orson Wells. *Seven Miles from Alcatraz* was Dmytryk's first film at the studio. Dmytryk worked primarily on second features until he unveiled the noir detective classic, *Murder, My Sweet* (1944), starring Dick Powell, which established him as a first-rate director and helped to shape RKO's film noir style. He stayed with RKO for three more years after that, ending with one of his most acclaimed films, the Oscar-nominated crime drama *Crossfire* (1947). His career was interrupted that year when the House Un-American Activities Committee (HUAC) named him one as of the *"Hollywood Ten."* Dmytryk left the country for England, where he directed two films before returning to the US; after six months, he renounced Communism and testified, naming names. Dmytryk worked steadily until his retirement in 1979 at the age of 71, though the shadow cast by his HUAC testimony never completely faded. His many high-profile films include *The Caine Mutiny* (1954), starring Humphrey Bogart; *Raintree County* (1957), starring Elizabeth Taylor; *The Young Lions* (1958), starring Marlon Brando; and *Mirage* (1965), starring Gregory Peck.

Writer JOHN D. KLORER's story about two unconventional war heroes was an interesting twist for a B movie promoting anti-Nazi war sentiments. Klorer penned a total of thirteen films before his untimely death at age 45 in 1951. They include the popular comedies *Guest Wife* (1945), with Claudette Colbert, and *Good Sam* (1948) with Gary Cooper and Ann Sheridan (who also appeared in *Alcatraz Island*).

Screenwriter JOSEPH KRUMGOLD wrote only twelve feature films, all second features, for Columbia, Republic, and RKO. *Seven Miles* is standard material, with a heavy emphasis on patriotism. The lighthouse captain is the voice of duty and loyalty who tries throughout the movie to convince Champ of his responsibility: "This is your war, whether you like it or not. It's being fought all over the world, by every storekeeper, preacher, ditch-digger, and even gangster." Krumgold's light-hearted dialogue for Champ and Jimbo keeps the movie entertaining, as when Jimbo tells off the annoying Stormy—"Now just a minute flounder-puss, spread out, you bother me."

Editor GEORGE CRONE's career at RKO started in 1933. Crone worked mostly on B movies, but two of his more familiar films are the Marx Brother's *Room Service* (1938) and the Robert Louis Stevenson adventure, *Swiss Family Robinson* (1940), directed by Edward Ludwig (*The Last Gangster*). He continued at RKO for ten years; *Seven Miles from Alcatraz* was one of his last films for the studio.

Cinematographer ROBERT DE GRASSE's first film was the John Ford silent, *Desperate Trails* (1921), made for Universal when he was 21 years old. Filming his way into the sound era, he joined RKO in the early '30s and was soon working with the studio's top directors and stars on films including *Alice Adams* (1935), *Stage Door* (1937), *Vivacious Lady* (1938), *Kitty Foyle* (1940), and *The Body Snatcher* (1945). *Seven Miles from Alcatraz* was a decidedly second feature, but benefits from De Grasse's handsome cinematography. De Grasse was one of the early pioneers in television, working on hit shows in the '50s and '60s, including *The Jack Benny Show*, *I Love Lucy*, and *The Dick Van Dyke Show*.

Composer ROY WEBB's music can be heard in over three hundred and fifty films spanning four decades. The spirited action score for *Seven Miles* plays an important part in keeping the scenes brisk and the tension high. Webb received seven Oscar nominations for his scores. His films include *My Favorite Wife* (1940), *I Married a Witch* (1942), *The Fighting Seabees* (1945), Dmytryk's *Murder, My Sweet* (1944), *Notorious* (1946), *Mighty Joe Young* (1949), and *Marty* (1955).

film poster

Of all the early Alcatraz film posters, *Seven Miles from Alcatraz* is the most dynamic. RKO was well known for mystery/thrillers and the film posters the studio produced were among the best at capturing the excitement and tension of the noir genre. Art director David Strumf guided RKO's talented artists through the '30s and '40s; the outstanding artwork he oversaw for the movie *King Kong* (1933) is among the best ever created. Many talented illustrators and designers had a hand in creating these wonderful posters, but most were unknown, and rarely signed their work.

Poster artists of the era had to capture the essence of the movie and the audience's attention, but were often not tied to the specifics of the narrative, and if the film had no major stars, there was less emphasis placed on creating realistic likenesses of the actors. The artwork for *Seven Miles* implies a thrilling story, and the overall sense of the plot is true, though not all the poster details appear in the movie itself.

TRAIN TO ALCATRAZ

Directed by
PHILIP FORD

REPUBLIC PICTURES
60 minutes, black and white

CAST

Don "Red" Barry	Doug Forbes
Janet Martin	Beatrice
William Phipps	Tommy Calligan
Roy Barcroft	Guard Grady
June Storey	Virginia Marley
Jane Darwell	Aunt Ella
Milburn Stone	Bart Kanin
Chester Clute	Conductor Yelvington
Ralph Dunn	US Marshal Mark Stevens
Richard Irving	Andy Anders
John Alvin	Nick
Michael Carr	Marty Mason
Marc Krah	Slip Mahaffey
Denver Pyle	Hutch Hutchins
Iron Eyes Cody	Geronimo
Bobby Stone	Hollister
Guard Reeves	Kenneth MacDonald

CREATIVE

Producer	Lou Brock
Screenplay	Gerald Geraghty
Cinematography	Reggie Lanning
Editing	Harold Minter
Art Direction	Fred A. Ritter
Set Decoration	John McCarthy Jr., George Milo
Musical Direction	Morton Scott

TRAIN TO
ALCATRAZ

starring
DONALD BARRY
JANET MARTIN
WILLIAM PHIPPS

with ROY BARCROFT • JUNE STOREY
JANE DARWELL • MILBURN STONE
Directed by PHILIP FORD • • •
ORIGINAL SCREEN PLAY BY GERALD GERAGHTY

A
REPUBLIC
PICTURE

THE STORY

A train speeds across the country heading toward its final destination, California and US Penitentiary Alcatraz Island. The first car is full of convicts shackled to one another with leg irons. US Marshal Stevens and four Alcatraz correctional officers, led by 20-year veteran Grady are on board to guard the prisoners and protect passengers in the other cars. Alcatraz's reputation as an escape-proof prison is well known and the convicts are nervously talking about how they can escape the train before it's too late. Tough Doug Forbes is planning something, and big-shot gangster Bart Kanin is plotting his own escape.

The train stops in New Mexico to pick up Tommy Calligan, who's accompanied by a federal officer. A young woman, Beatrice, and her Aunt Ella are waiting for the same train. Beatrice smiles at Tommy until she notices that he's handcuffed. "All of you men are on your way to Alcatraz because you've been constant trouble elsewhere." officer Grady tells Tommy, whose escape attempt from his former prison landed him on the train to Alcatraz. As they go down the aisle, Grady explains each man's criminal past and why Alcatraz will be their last stop, where escape is impossible. Tommy sees Bart Kanin, the man who set him up for killing a police officer and put him on the train to Alcatraz. He confronts Kanin and vows revenge. Tommy takes a seat next to Forbes, who becomes his ally.

Officer Grady goes to the passenger car, where Kanin's girlfriend Virginia manages to slip a key into Grady's coat pocket that will open Kanin's leg irons. Virginia marks Grady's collar with lipstick to signal Kanin. When Grady goes back to the convict car, Kanin sees the lipstick and steals the key from Grady. In the meantime, Forbes puts his own escape plan into action. When he's taken to the bathroom by a guard, he cuts off the electricity and steals the guard's gun, then takes over the car and holds three guards hostage. Tommy sees his chance and attacks Kanin, but Kanin, who has a gun, shoots Tommy in the arm, and is about to finish him off when Forbes rushes in and kills Kanin. Forbes threatens the marshal outside the convict's car—unless the train stops, he'll start killing guards. The marshal refuses, and Forbes executes one of the guards.

Meanwhile, back in Tommy's hometown, the police find evidence that Bart Kanin's henchman killed the police officer, not Tommy. They arrest the henchman and quickly send a letter to intercept the train and free Tommy.

Not knowing Kanin is dead, Virginia pulls a gun on the conductor and forces him to stop the train. Forbes jumps off, but the marshal kills him, and then regains control of the convicts. Beatrice is tending Tommy's injury when the telegram announcing Tommy's innocence arrives. Alcatraz Island appears on the screen as the film ends.

TRAIN OF PRISONERS ON BARGE TO ALCATRAZ

THE INSIDE SCOOP

Train to Alcatraz is a classic Republic feature. It's fast-paced, stars one of their action heroes (Don Barry), and uses a team of company talent. Though the film hinges on Alcatraz's well-known reputation, it rarely escapes the confines of the train, except for outdoor shots of the huge black locomotive charging through the countryside toward California, its engine bursting with power, its stack billowing out gusts of smoke. The dialogue has fun moments, but the acting is standard, with the exception of the film's star Don Barry as a hotheaded tough guy and June Storey as a gangster's "moll." What is surprising is how rough the action is—when a guard held hostage by Forbes is shot point blank, it's startling. In Hollywood's stylish gangster tradition, the prisoners wear white shirts and suits, (most sport ties), the good guys win in the end, and it all adds up to an action-packed hour at the movies.

In an early scene, the terror of Alcatraz is made clear. As the train speeds along, Nick, one of the prisoners, hears things in the rotating sounds of the train wheels: "Escape, escape before it's too late, escape, escape before it's too late." He becomes frightened and starts screaming, "They're taking us to Alcatraz. We'll be there for the rest of our lives. It's a fortress. It's a fortress, I tell you, sitting in the middle of the bay with tides all around you waiting to grab you down." Nick never makes it to the terrifying Rock. He grabs a guard's gun and holds the conductor hostage, but is shot attempting to escape.

FIRST TRAIN OF PRISONERS ARRIVES ON ALCATRAZ, AUGUST 1934

the studio: REPUBLIC PICTURES

Republic Pictures was known for their popular low-budget B pictures as well as *"Dick Tracy," "Lone Ranger," "Zorro,"* and other Saturday-afternoon serials. Westerns were their mainstay, and starred action heroes like John Wayne, Roy Rogers, and Gene Autry. Founded by Herbert Yates in 1935, Republic Pictures emerged from a consolidation of several minor "poverty row" studios. Republic introduced choreographed fight scenes, and was known for their special effects, explosions, and simulating superheroes' ability to fly. Republic ran like a factory; its company of talented directors, writers, and creative staff fashioned hundreds of inexpensive, quickly made, and predictable stories for their well-known stars. The studio produced a few memorable feature films, notably *Sands of Iwo Jima* (1949) and the Oscar-winning John Ford classic, *The Quiet Man* (1952), both starring John Wayne. The company stopped production of serials in 1955, and ceased making movie-length films in 1959 when B pictures were no longer part of theater programming.

"Escape, escape before it's too late."

Crazed convict hearing message in train wheels on the way to Alcatraz.

ALCATRAZ: REEL TO REAL

In fact, trains were used to transport prisoners to Alcatraz. These cars were equipped with special features including steel bodies, steel-barred windows, and wire-screened cages from which the guards could see the full length of the car. Their trips across country avoided heavily populated areas. The first train to Alcatraz arrived at Tiburon on August 22, 1934, from UPS Atlanta. From there, it was transferred onto a barge and towed to the island. When all prisoners were accounted for and safely on Alcatraz, Warden Johnston notified the US Attorney General by telegram: "Fifty-three crates furniture from Atlanta received in good condition –installed–no breakage." This train was a "special" (or unscheduled) train that consisted of a locomotive, tender, and three passenger cars. It was the biggest shipment of men ever sent to the island at one time. Convicts were usually transported in small numbers (sometimes even singly) and traveled on regular passenger cars, but under tight security, shackled, and escorted by federal marshals.

As newcomer Tommy boards the train, a seasoned Alcatraz guard aptly describes the prison: "Take a good look at the scenery. Last chance you're gonna have for a long time. There's scenery there too, only it ain't close enough to get a good look at. Lights off in the distance, maybe a ship going by on the other side of the bay. You're lucky if you see anything though, with the fog rolling in most of the time, makes it kind of cold and gloomy. You'll find out what I mean."

"I'd rather have three months on my own, than twenty years on the Rock."

Criminal Doug Forbes in *Train to Alcatraz*

STARRING

DON "RED" BARRY (Forbes) starred in a series of Republic Westerns, most notably as Red Ryder in the *"Adventures of Red Ryder"* serial (from which he took his name). Barry is the most vibrant of the cast, bringing a sense of urgency to his desperation to get off the train. In the '50s, Barry began a career in supporting roles in films and television shows, including *I'll Cry Tomorrow* (1955), *Walk on the Wild Side* (1962), *The Shakiest Gun in the West* (1968), and *The Swarm* (1978). In a career that spanned six decades—from the 1930s to the 1980s—Barry appeared in over one hundred and forty films.

WILLIAM PHIPPS (Tommy Calligan) had a long career in the movies and in hundreds of television shows. Phipps was cast in many of the early Westerns, but became known for his roles in 1950s sci-fi classics, including *Five* (1951), *Cat Women of the Moon* and *War of the Worlds* (both 1953), and *Snow Creatures* (1954). He appeared in *The Man of the Eiffel Tower* (1950), *Executive Suite* (1954), and as Teddy Roosevelt in television's *Eleanor and Franklin* (1976). Phipps, who did voiceover work throughout his career, was immortalized as the voice of Prince Charming in Disney's 1950 animated classic *Cinderella*.

ROY BARCROFT (Grady) made over three hundred films, usually portraying a convincing villain or venerable sheriff in Republic Westerns. He often worked with *Train to Alcatraz* director Philip Ford, as well as with Gene Autry. Barcroft's familiar films include *Man with a Star* and *Oklahoma* (both 1955), and *The Reivers* (1969).

MILBURN STONE (Bart Kanin) is most often remembered for his Emmy-Award-winning role as Dr. Galen Adams in the television series *Gunsmoke* (1955–1975). Stone's suave looks suited his sophisticated mob-boss part Bart Kanin in *Train to Alcatraz*. Stone worked as a character actor from the 1930s through the 1950s, often cast as the handsome and reliable captain, lieutenant, or inspector.

JUNE STOREY (Virginia) appeared in two Alcatraz films. Her first was in 1945 as Kit Norton in *Road to Alcatraz* (1945). In *Train*, Storey is beautiful, conniving, and deadly as the villainous blond who seduces Tommy to commit a crime. Storey starred in many Gene Autry films of the '30s and '40s.

CHESTER CLUTE (Conductor), a veteran of more than two hundred films, provides subtle comedic moments on the Alcatraz train. He was delightful in the classic comedies *The More the Merrier* (1943), *Arsenic and Old Lace* (1944), and *Guest Wife* (1945). Clute was often cast in small, amusing, and un-credited roles, such as a hotel clerk, apartment manager, or bank teller with memorable names like Higgenbotham or Adolphe Bietjelboer.

BEHIND THE SCENES

Director PHILIP FORD came from a distinguished film family. Son of director and actor Francis Ford and nephew of renowned director John Ford, Philip Ford began his career as an actor working primarily for his father in silent films. He moved to directing with the 1945 crime film, *The Tiger Woman*. Though Ford also directed horror and mystery films, he's best known for his Westerns, often working with his *Train to Alcatraz* team as well as casting his father Francis in small roles.

Screenwriter GERALD GERAGHTY wrote screenplays for many Gene Autry and *"Lone Ranger"* serials, as well as early Dorothy Lamour films, *The Jungle Princess* (1936) and *Her Jungle Love* (1938). Geraghty has fun with Alcatraz references in his *Train to Alcatraz* screenplay. A guard describes one of the convicts on the train to Alcatraz: "Young fellow is Hollister, bad habit of robbing the mail, gonna get him a nice Alcatraz haircut."

Editor HOWARD MINTER joined Republic Pictures in 1944 on the jungle adventure *The Tiger Woman* and he continued at the studio working on over fifty of their popular Western and action pictures including *King of the Forest Rangers* (1946), *Bandit King of Texas* (1949), and *Phantom Stallion* (1954).

Cinematographer REGGIE LANSING's joined Republic Pictures in 1936 when he was forty-three, and worked on over one hundred films during his twenty-six years at the studio, including *Rosie the Riveter* (1944), *Calendar Girl* (1947), Gene Autry and Roy Rogers Westerns, and John Wayne's *The Sands of Iwo Jima* (1949), and *Thunderbirds* (1954), about an Oklahoma National Guard unit composed mainly of Native Americans during WWII.

Musical Director MORTON SCOTT's score for *Train to Alcatraz* is well suited to the action, and appropriately overwrought when paired with footage of the terrifying Rock. He was nominated for Oscars twice—both in 1945 for scoring of a musical (*Hitchhike to Happiness*) and a drama (*Flame of Barbary Coast*), a John Wayne vehicle set in San Francisco during the 1906 earthquake. Morton started his career in 1942 at Republic pictures, working on *Sunset Serenade* starring Roy Rogers, and continued there until 1950, directing music for over 125 movies.

Costume Designer ADELE PALMER worked for Republic Pictures for seventeen years, creating costumes for more than one hundred fifty films. She costumed countless Westerns as well as crime, war, and drama films, including Orson Welles' *Macbeth* (1948) and John Ford's *The Quiet Man* (1952). When Republic Pictures abandoned the film business for television, Palmer went to work with other studios. She created her most noteworthy work in '50s melodramas including *The Long Hot Summer* (1958), *Peyton Place* (1959), and *The Best of Everything* (1959), for which she received an Oscar nomination.

film poster

Republic Pictures stars Don "Red" Barry and Roy Barcroft are featured in the classic B movie poster for *Train to Alcatraz*. Lacking big name stars to sell the film, B movies needed to entice its audiences in one quick image. Though the drawings are awkward, the design basic (type on top with picture below), and renderings of the film's stars rough, the overall effect gets right to the film's dangerous storyline: Criminals take over a train headed to Alcatraz. (Note the determined stares between prisoner and officer and the tense grip of the criminal's claw-like hand.) The poster's yellow, red, and blue color scheme is similar to many of the gangster films of the time, especially those made by Republic Pictures. Republic was known for its artists' distinctive watercolor technique and strong use of black, most noticeable here in the Alcatraz title.

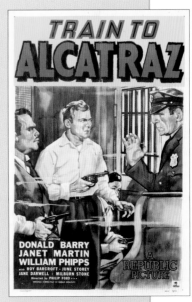

TRAIN CAR WITH PRISONERS

EXPERIMENT ALCATRAZ

Directed by
EDWARD L. CAHN

RKO PICTURES
57 minutes, Black and White

CAST

John Howard	Dr. Ross Williams
Joan Dixon	Joan McKenna
Walter Kingsford	Dr. J. P. Finley
Lynne Carter	Ethel Ganz
Robert Shayne	Barry Morgan
Kim Spalding	Duke Shaw
Sam Scar	Eddie Ganz
Kenneth MacDonald	Col. Harris
Dick Cogan	Dan Staley
Frank Cady	Max Henry

CREATIVE

Producer	Edward L. Cahn
Story	George W. George
	George F. Slavin
Screenplay	Orville H. Hampton
Cinematography	Jackson Rose
Editing	Philip Cahn
Art Direction	Boris Leven
Set Decoration	Otto Siegel
Original Music	Irving Gertz

THE STORY

Five Alcatraz "lifers" agree to undergo atomic radiation treatment in exchange for their freedom—that is, if they survive. The inmates are escorted from Alcatraz to a medical facility in the Presidio of San Francisco. One by one, the prisoner/patients are exposed to radioactive rays streaming down from an overhead lamp. A team of medical experts watch behind glass panels as the prisoners writhe in pain, and then settle into unconsciousness as the rays subside.

In the recovery room, army nurse Joan McKenna accidentally drops a pair of scissors on prisoner Barry Morgan's bed. When he awakes, he finds the scissors, and in a crazed state, kills fellow prisoner Eddie Ganz. The radiation treatment is blamed for Morgan's outburst and the experiment is declared a disaster. As a result, all the prisoners are set free and Nurse McKenna is relieved of duty. The developer of the isotope, Dr. Ross Williams, cannot understand Morgan's violent reaction and teams up with negligent Nurse McKenna (whose ill brother is in desperate need of treatment) to search for the truth.

Dr. Williams goes to see the DA, who tells him that the case is closed, and then visits Morgan, whose refusal to help makes the doctor suspicious that he might have murdered Ganz. Not knowing what else to do, Williams and McKenna visit Alcatraz Island, where Warden Keaton brings in inmate Max Henry to speak with them. Henry came up from Leavenworth with Morgan and Ganz (for attempting an escape), but claims the two men were friends, in fact, he tells a story about how Morgan saved Eddie's life. Feeling discouraged, Williams and McKenna are about to leave when Henry, who has a collection of discarded postcards from other inmates, asks his visitors if they'd like to see them. Realizing how much it would mean to the lonely convict, Dr. Williams agrees to look at them. As he shuffles through the cards, he notices one written by an Ethel Ganz to Eddie Ganz with a picture of a house by Lake Tahoe. Delighted to finally have a lead, Williams and McKenna head out of Alcatraz and promise to send Henry a postcard every week.

The amateur sleuths travel to Tahoe and track down Ethel, who, they find out, is Eddie's stepdaughter. Williams goes to the house with Ethel. Alone with the doctor, Ethel pulls out a gun and reveals that she's been in cahoots with Morgan to find out where Eddie hid his money. Once Ethel discovered the dough in the mantle of the Lake Tahoe house, Eddie became expendable. The experiment offered them the perfect solution, as Morgan could pretend to be crazy as an excuse to murder him. Suddenly, Morgan shows up and kills Dr. Williams.

All seems lost until old Dr. Finley devises a scheme. He convinces Morgan to undergo a follow-up treatment, unaware it's a placebo. When Dr. Finley informs Morgan that he knows the truth, Morgan pretends to be crazy again from the treatment, and tries to kill him, but three orderlies (hiding behind a curtain) jump out and rescue the old doctor. The truth is out, Dr. Williams' radiation treatment is proven a success, and negligent nurse McKenna's brother is saved.

VIEW OF ALCATRAZ FROM PRESIDIO OF SAN FRANCISCO

THE INSIDE SCOOP

Producer-director Edward L. Cahn brought his own brand of filmmaking to RKO in 1950 in two films, *Destination Murder* and *Experiment Alcatraz*, casting character actors and second leads in these quickly produced, inexpensive movies. Cahn was known for his ability to create small energetic films that allowed the studios to turn a quick profit. In *Experiment Alcatraz*, Cahn takes a hot 1950s topic (radioactivity), an interesting premise (experiments on prisoners), and using what seems like a purposefully flat style (sober script, stiff acting, no-nonsense scenes), creates one of his many unique films. An entertaining score by Irving Gertz hits all the right musical clichés, keeping the story moving along at a lively pace. In one early scene in the warden's office, Cahn offers us a close-up of each of the five Alcatraz prisoners. One by one the camera pans the men's hardened faces as they react to undergoing an experimental radioactive treatment with uncertain results. It's a brief but moving moment that Cahn captures in his simple and telling style. When we see these same men (excluding the murderer) a short time later, appearing well dressed, groomed, and acting like model citizens, one wonders if Alcatraz actually incarcerates criminals. This is reinforced when we later meet a meek, postcard-collecting inmate who is treated with fatherly affection by the warden. If one can enjoy seeing radioactive isotope rays spray down from an overhead lamp, and an absent-minded nurse drop scissors on a convict's bed, this movie is quite entertaining.

the studio: RKO

Between 1943 and 1946, RKO experienced it greatest financial successes, with films including, *Hitler's Children* and *Behind the Rising Sun* (both 1943 and directed by Edward Dmytryk, who was also the director for *Seven Miles from Alcatraz)*; *The Bells of St. Mary* (1945), and *Notorious* (1946). After the war, RKO's fortunes dropped significantly, and by 1947, they were heading for financial trouble. In 1948, multi-millionaire Howard Hughes acquired the controlling share of RKO; Hughes was a ruthless and erratic leader and his tenure was marked by confusion and mismanagement. By the end of the 1950s, RKO Pictures ceased to exist. Lucille Ball and Desi Arnaz bought the studio for their own production company, Desilu, where they filmed the successful *"I Love Lucy"* series (1951–1957) among other shows.

ALCATRAZ: REEL TO REAL

The only Alcatraz-related movie scenes take place in the fictitious warden's office. Alcatraz and the Presidio of San Francisco (today, both are part of the Golden Gate National Parks, managed by the National Park Service and—in the case of the Presidio—the Presidio Trust) played small but pivotal roles in the overall picture, giving the film its unique storyline and compelling title and connecting a federal penitentiary to a military experiment. In the 1950s, Alcatraz was still in active service as a federal prison and was completely off-limits to filmmakers, and the Presidio was an active military base; however, filmmakers were allowed to shoot a few short sequences on the Presidio's main parade ground when the convicts arrive for their tests. The movie gives viewers a great opportunity to see some of the Presidio's splendid buildings in their heyday.

STARRING

JOHN HOWARD (Dr. Ross Williams) was a popular Hollywood actor well known in the 1930s for playing Captain Hugh Chesterton "Bulldog" Drummond in Herman C. McNeile's mystery series. Howard's role as the heroic doctor who dies in search of the truth echoes his real-life accomplishments as both a Phi Beta Kappa graduate and WWII war hero who received the Navy Cross and the *Croix de Guerre* for valor. Howard played Katherine Hepburn's rich fiancé George Kittridge, whom she left at the altar (for Cary Grant) in *The Philadelphia Story* (1940). His most memorable role was playing Ronald Coleman's brother in Frank Capra's classic *Lost Horizon* (1937). His films include *Father Takes a Wife*, (1941), *Isle of Missing Men* (1942), and *The High and the Mighty* (1954). Curiously, Howard's last film was the 1975 *Capone*, starring Ben Gazzara, in which he played Alcatraz warden James A. Johnston.

WALTER KINGSFORD (Dr. Finley) was a character actor who made over one hundred films and television appearances. As in *Experiment Alcatraz*, Kingsford's portly stature and kind face were well suited for medical-profession roles. Throughout his career, he was cast as a doctor twenty times in such films as *Captains Courageous* (1937), *Carefree* (1938), *My Favorite Blonde* (1942), and *Mr. Skeffington* (1944). He also made multiple appearances as Dr. Walter Carew in the *"Dr. Kildare"* series of the '30s and '40s.

ROBERT SHAYNE's (Barry Morgan) villainous performance in *Experiment Alcatraz* stands out amidst some rather stiff acting. A well-known Hollywood character actor whose career stretched from the '30s to the '70s, he worked at Warner Brothers from 1942 to 1946 in B-Westerns and in supporting roles in more prestigious films, including *Christmas in Connecticut* and *San Antonio* (both 1945). Many may remember him as Inspector William (Bill) Henderson in the popular 1950s television series, *"Adventures of Superman."*

JOAN DIXON (Lt. Nurse Joan McKenna) had a short Hollywood career. She made ten films at RKO, all average B productions. As the negligent nurse McKenna, Dixon is uncompromisingly dull, though her flat acting fits well into director Cahn's style.

FRANK CADY (Max Henry) portrays a gentle Alcatraz prisoner who finds comfort in the discarded postcards received by other prisoners. This appropriately hokey character was perfectly played by Cady, who became familiar to TV viewers as the irascible Sam Drucker in *Petticoat Junction* (1963–1970), as well as in *Green Acres* (1965–1973) and *The Beverly Hillbillies* (1968–1969). In 1950, the year *Experiment Alcatraz* was released; Cady could be seen (briefly) in thirteen films playing (among other things), a bartender in *DOA*, a night clerk in *The Asphalt Jungle*, and a timid engagement party guest in *Father of the Bride*.

"The only chance to prove that the radiation wasn't responsible for your father's death is to show that Morgan had a motive *for...*

Dr. Ross Williams, developer
of the radioactive isotope,
Experiment Alcatraz

BEHIND THE SCENES

Director and Producer EDWARD L. CAHN was an innovative filmmaker, achieving fame after his death for a remarkable body of low budget "cult" films. Cahn made over one hundred films including the '50s sci-fi classics, *Zombies of Mora Tau*, *Invasion of the Saucer Men*, and *Voodoo Woman* (all 1957), and *Invisible Invader* (1959). Brooklyn-born Cahn started his career at Universal Studios, becoming chief film editor working on major releases including *The Man who Laughs* (1928), *Broadway* (1929), and the Oscar winning *All Quiet on the Western Front* (1931, uncredited). He began directing in 1931, and a year later released the thrilling *Law and Order* (1932), starring Walter Huston and Harry Carey (*King of Alcatraz*), based on a script co-authored by John Huston. Throughout the '30s and '40s Cahn worked at most of the major studios on crime and action thrillers. In 1955, Cahn made the hit *Creature with the Atom Brain* for Columbia, followed by other popular titles including *Runaway Daughters*, *Girls in Prison*, *The She-Creature*, *Flesh and the Spur*, and *Silent Fear* (all 1956). In 1958 Cahn released two memorable thrillers: *It! The Terror from Beyond Space* and *Curse of the Faceless Man*. He was at the helm of the cold-war espionage thriller *Hong Kong Confidential* (1958), with Gene Barry as a lounge-singer spy; the crime drama *Guns, Girls, and Gangsters* (1959), starring Mamie Van Doren; and the co-ed prison film, *Riot in Juvenile Prison* (1959). Cahn has influenced many filmmakers, including George Romero and Ridley Scott.

Story writers GEORGE W. GEORGE and **GEORGE F. SLAVIN** and **Screenwriter ORVILLE H. HAMPTON** took advantage of the 1950s obsession with atomic energy when they created *Experiment Alcatraz*. George and Slavin wrote many B movies together, including another atomic energy film, *The Rocket Man* (1954) with social comic Lenny Bruce, about a boy who finds a ray gun that forces people to tell the truth. Hampton wrote scripts for movies and television, penning many of Edward L. Cahn's pictures. Hampton won an Oscar nomination (with Raphael Hayes) for *One Potato, Two Potato* (1964), an insightful story of interracial marriage starring Barbara Barrie and Bernie Hamilton.

Cinematographer JACKSON ROSE's first job was for the "King of the Movies", silent film star Francis X. Bushman, on *One Wonderful Night* (1914). Rose, only 18 years old, was working at the pioneering Essanay Film Manufacturing Company. Among his more than one hundred and forty films and shorts were the gangster biography, *Dillinger* (1945); a dozen Edward L. Cahn films; and during his years at MGM, many of their best *"Our Gang"* comedies.

Art Director BORIS LEVEN, nominated for nine Oscars and winning in 1961 for *West Side Story*, was one of the most illustrious members of the team. Leven served as art director or production designer on some of Hollywood's biggest films, including *Alexander's Ragtime Band* (1938), *Giant* (1956), *The Sound of Music* (1965), *Star* (1968), *New York, New York* (1977), and *The Color of Money* (1986). It is difficult to compare Leven's work on these major films with the simple and hokey *Experiment Alcatraz*, though his art direction well suits Cahn's particular aesthetic.

film poster

In the wonderful hand-painted poster art for *Experiment Alcatraz*, the signature RKO quality is very much intact, even though the studio itself was headed toward extinction. Its style echoed that of many posters of the era—exciting and dangerous—and representations of stars John Howard and Robert Shayne are excellent. A scene in the bottom right shows a man being attacked behind bars, conveying the violence and fear that a radioactive experiment might cause, though no actual scenes of men behind bars are included in the film. Marketing text, *Radioactive Drug Test an Alibi for Murder!* blazes across the top in bold yellow type, piquing moviegoers' curiosity. The poster was produced and distributed by National Screen Services (NSS), who worked with many studios to promote their films; the number "51/28", located in the poster's lower left-hand corner, indicates that it was produced in 1951 and was NSS's 28th movie poster that year. *Experiment Alcatraz* was released on Nov. 21, 1950, and this poster was produced sometime early the following year.

WARDEN'S OFFICE, CIRCA 1961

PRESIDIO OF SAN FRANCISCO: MONTGOMERY STREET BARRACKS

"Now listen Doc, I spent years in the stir trying to get that money, dough that Eddie chiseled from me in the first place...when this experiment came along I saw my chance and I killed him."

Alcatraz Inmate Barry Morgan, *Experiment Alcatraz*

FROM NEWSPAPER HEADLINES TO MOVIE MARQUEES

Screenwriters working on early Alcatraz films had to use newspaper and magazine articles to find out what little was known publicly about the island prison. Luckily, the infamous Alcatraz often made headline news, which, in turn, helped the prison build its reputation as the toughest in America as it gave filmmakers sensational storylines for their movies. For example, on December 16, 1937, the Portland Press Herald's headlines announced that two Alcatraz inmates, Theodore Cole and Ralph Roe, had escaped.

The first Alcatraz films, *Alcatraz Island* and *The Last Gangster*, both released in 1937 (November 6 and 12, respectively), were written before anyone had fled the "escape-proof" prison. And while in 1938, *King of Alcatraz* advertises an escape, the inmate actually gets away after he's taken off the island and is en route to a hospital. Then, in 1940, *House Across the Bay* became the first film released after Cole and Roe's 1937 flight to show a prisoner actually escaping from the island (the film's portrayal of the event was ludicrous--see *House Across the Bay*, p. 39, for details). All in all, another example of the way Hollywood used—and altered—historical fact.

Though built on a tiny island in the middle of San Francisco Bay, Alcatraz was known throughout the country as America's maximum security prison, a place where only the most dangerous men were incarcerated. This excerpt is from the *Portland Press Herald*, published clear across the US in the state of Maine, 2,717 miles away.

Portland Press Herald

PORTLAND, MAINE, FRIDAY MORNING, DECEMBER 17, 1937

Two Disappear From "Escape-Proof" Alcatr

Coast Guard Craft And Police Boats Cruise Around Island In Search

THEODORE COLE, RALPH ROE ARE THE MISSING INMATES

San Francisco Bay Shrouded With Heavy Fog---Water Calm, Tide Running Toward Mainland When Break Discovered

San Francisco Bay Shrouded with Heavy Fog

San Francisco, Dec. 16 – (UP) – Two long-term convicts disappeared tonight from the Federal Government's "escape-proof" prison on Alcatraz Island in San Francisco Bay. Coast Guard cutters and police boats swept the bay for the two—Theodore Cole and Ralph Roe—but were hampered by a thick fog over the island, which is a quarter of a mile from shore. None has ever escaped from the prison which houses the Country's most desperate criminals. Warden James A. Johnston called upon police to search waterfront areas for the men in the possibility they had managed to reach shore. Six Coast Guard cutters and a police launch conducted a systematic search about the island. Officers pointed out that if the men had leaped into the water, they would have been aided by the calm weather and a high incoming tide, which was running toward the mainland and other islands densely covered by underbrush. A Coast Guard officer, returning to his base temporarily from the island patrol, revealed that it was considered possible that Cole and Roe had been met by a boat off the Rocky Island. As darkness fell, the tide changed to ebb and began flowing at a rate of seven knots toward the Golden Gate, several miles West of the prison. Officials said that any one attempting to swim in that tide would be swept out to sea.

So thick was the fog surrounding the island when the two men were first reported missing that ferry boats were moving at a greatly reduced speed. Three Coast Guard cutters were concentrated at the north end of the island in the belief that Roe and Cole might be hiding under rocks, possibly waiting for nightfall. The prison launch *McDonald* moved slowly around the island's rocky walls, unable to get in close because of high tides. It was not known definitely what time the disappearance of the prisoners was discovered, but after 2 p.m. (PST) Coast Guard boats were seen concentrating around the island and Johnston telephoned his report of the disappearance to Washington at 3:30 p.m. (PST).

No one has ever succeeded in scaling the high walls without being seen by guards. At ebb tide, jagged rocks rise above the water, making it impossible for a man to jump from a wall. But at high tide these rocks are covered, and a man might plunge from a wall into safe water. Then he would have a long flight in a treacherous current to reach shore. Only one previous escape attempt from the American "Devil's Island" is on record and the convict who made the attempt was killed. But the island where the nation's most desperate and spectacular prisoners are housed under stern discipline has known two convict rebellions, stabbings, a suicide, and an attack on Johnston.

Johnston assured Federal Prison Director James V. Bennett in the telephone report that "every effort" is being made to locate the fugitives, and said that the Coast Guard and other law enforcement agencies had been called into the search. Johnston reported to Bennett that a "pea soup" fog began enveloping the island early today and that when a checkup of the convicts was made toward dusk that the two men were found to be missing.

PORTLAND PRESS HERALD. 1937

POSTERS: National Screen Services

In the burgeoning early years of the film industry, subsidiary companies developed to support the lucrative movie business. In the '20s, a company called National Screen Services (NSS) took on the production and distribution of movie trailers for most of the major studios. The movie studios initially produced and distributed their own posters, but by the late '40s, many were using NSS to manufacture and distribute their posters, lobby cards, and other advertising materials. RKO was among the first to employ their services and in 1940, signed a five-year contract with NSS. The *Seven Miles from Alcatraz* poster is marked with the NSS name and copyright. In the lower right, the poster is numbered 42/550, signifying that the poster was produced in 1942 and was the 550th movie poster they produced that year. The film was released in early November 1942, among the later posters that year, which gives an idea of how many movies NSS handled for the studios; only Paramount, MGM, and RKO were using NSS's services in 1942. Others joined later in the decade. Morgan Lithographers in Cleveland, Ohio, printed the *Seven Miles* poster. The size of the poster is 27" x 41" and is referred to as a one-sheet. The one-sheet has been the predominant size for the movie poster since the early days of the film industry, and remains so today, almost ninety years later.

PRISON FILMS

The public has always been fascinated by prisons, as evident in the close to 1.5 million people from around the world who visit the abandoned prison on Alcatraz each year. The stories of inmates, wardens, guards, and the prison system have been dramatized, idealized, and completely fictionalized by Hollywood. An early entry in the genre, *The Big House* (1930), with Wallace Beery was a tough and stark portrait of life behind bars. In 1937, *Alcatraz Island* brought the island prison into the cinematic lexicon. These films (and others that followed) set their stories on Alcatraz because it was known as the toughest prison in America, but they didn't probe or even show much of prison life. *Riot in Cell Block 11* (1954) directed by Don Siegel, was a unique movie; filmed in a documentary-style, it presented the unjustness in our country's prison system. Most offer little insight into our correctional system (though the prison industry is, shamefully, one of the fastest growing in our society), but the harshness of life behind bars is seldom underplayed, and many do offer an empathetic understanding of our criminal population. Through the decades, the best of these films have depicted characters whose lives are being shaped by their prison experience, including Burt Lancaster in *Birdman of Alcatraz* (1962), Paul Newman in *Cool Hand Luke* (1967), Dustin Hoffman and Steve McQueen in *Papillon* (1973), Clint Eastwood in *Escape from Alcatraz* (1979), and Tim Robbins and Morgan Freeman in *The Shawshank Redemption* (1994).

VIOLENCE in early cinema

Violence in gangster films reached a peak with *Scarface* (1932), starring Paul Muni as the Capone-like Antonio "Tony" Camonte. The film had a body count of 43, and the Motion Picture Production Code refused to give the film its seal of approval. The title was changed to *Scarface: Shame of a Nation*, but local censors ended up cutting a number of scenes. In 1933, the National Committee for the Study of Social Values published a study on crime, claiming that gangster movies were educating a new group of criminals. Religious groups, the Order of the Sons of Italy (a US group), and the International Association of Chiefs of Police all pressured Hollywood to end movie violence.

To prevent government censorship, the movie industry agreed to enforce its own Production Code, which it had been ignoring. Then, in 1934, when the FBI killed John Dillinger, Pretty Boy Floyd, and Baby Face Nelson, the industry took its cue from this headline news and began creating films whose heroes were special government agents. The first film was *G Men* (1935), starring James Cagney. Similar films followed, but many ended up as violent as their predecessors, and the studios were again forced to tone down their pictures to avoid government censorship.

THE B MOVIE

When the Great Depression of the 1930s hit Hollywood, and box-office tallies started to dwindle, the studios, in an effort to entice audiences back to the theaters, began offering low-budget supporting films known as B movies. After RKO and Lowes implemented these second features into all their theaters, the other studios followed suit. Each studio had a B division which reflected their style, (Warner Bros., B gangster films; Paramount, B melodramas); they used up-and-coming directors and actors, or offered older actors work in the twilight of their careers. Directors Edward Dmytryk (*Seven Miles from Alcatraz*) and Robert Florey (*King of Alcatraz*); young actors Robert Preston, Anthony Quinn, and Dennis Morgan (*King of Alcatraz*); and older stars Jack Holt (*Passport Alcatraz*) and John Howard (*Experiment Alcatraz*) all worked in B movies. Republic Pictures (*Train to Alcatraz*) was known for its serials and B movies (many with a Western theme). When the Supreme Court forced studios to divest themselves of their theaters or be in violation of anti-trust laws, the B movie began to fade. Though the proliferation of television ended the need for B movies, it provided work for much of the talent who made them.

1937

1937

1938

1940

1941

1943

1948

1950

1962

1967

1968

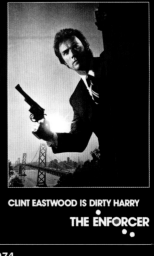

1974

1979

1995

1996

BUILDING THE ALCATRAZ MYTH, ONE MOVIE AT A TIME

■ ■ ■ ■ ■ ■ ■ ■ ■ ■ ■

MOVIES SHOWN TO INMATES ON ALCATRAZ IN 1943
(partial list)

January 3	Features: *Eagle Squadron, The Body Disappears*
January 31	Features: *For Me and My Gal, Moscow Strikes Back*
February 7	Educational: *Women in Defense*
February 21	Features: *The Battle of Midway*
March 14	Educational: *Sky Dancers of Papantla*
March 28	Features: *You Were Never Lovelier*
April 4	Educational: *War in the Pacific*
April 25	Features: *Holiday Inn, My Favorite Blonde*
May 9	Educational: *Winning Your Wings*
May 30	Features: *Panama Hattie*
June 13	Educational: *San Francisco Reception Madame Kai Shek*
June 20	Features: *The Palm Beach Story*
July 4	Features: *Star Spangled Rhythm*
July 11	Educational: *Divide and Conquer*
August 8	Features: *The Major and the Minor*
August 22	Educational: *People of Russia*
September 5	Features: *Stand by for Action*
September 26	Educational: *March of Time, "Show Business at War"*
October 10	Features: *The Road to Morocco, Hit Parade of 1943*
October 31	Educational: *"Sniffer Soldiers"*
November 7	Features: *Stage Door Canteen*
November 21	Features: *I Married a Witch*
December 12	Educational: *Rear Gunner*
December 19	Features: Dickens' *Christmas Carol*
December 25	Features: *Happy Go Lucky*

According to Alcatraz Captain of the Guard Phil Bergen, early on, movies were only shown during holidays, but the frequency gradually increased, and finally, films were offered every other Sunday. Westerns, Shirley Temple, and Busby Berkeley were all popular. The authorities steered away from most romantic and political movies, as well as crime and detective films. Protestant chaplains selected films to be shown within set parameters, and the films were always viewed by the staff afterwards.

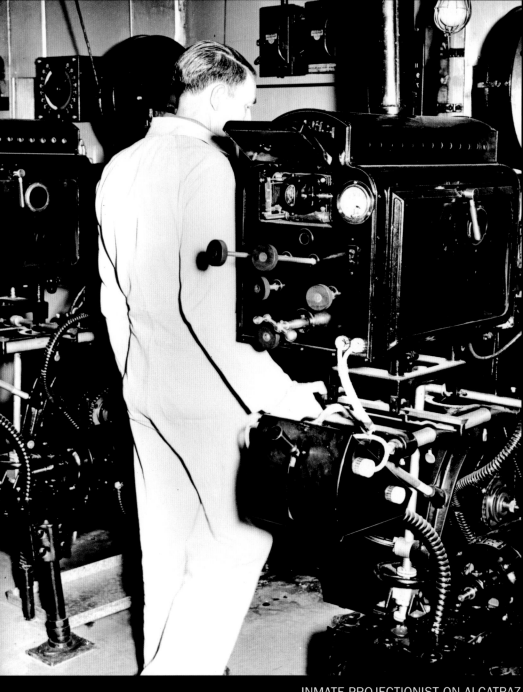

INMATE PROJECTIONIST ON ALCATRAZ

ALCATRAZ ESCAPES

April, 27, 1936—Joseph Bowers climbed fence in full view of guard and was shot and killed.

December 16, 1937—Ralph Roe and Theodore Cole sawed through window bar in Model Industries building, squeezed through, and disappeared.

May 23, 1938—James Lucas, Thomas Limerick, and Rufus Franklin clubbed Officer Royal Cline to death with hammer. Tower guard killed Limerick, wounded Franklin. Lucas captured.

January 13, 1939—Arthur "Doc" Barker, Dale Stamphill, Rufus McCain, William Martin, and Henri Young sawed through window bars in D-Block, scrambled to water's edge. Barker fatally wounded, others captured.

May 21, 1941—Joseph Cretzer, Sam Shockley, Arnold Kyle, and Lloyd Barkdoll overpowered guards in mat shop, but gave up after unsuccessful attempt to saw through window bars.

September 15, 1941—John Bayless slipped away from garbage detail near power-house, but was spotted in water and brought back.

April 14, 1943—Floyd Hamilton, Harold Brest, Fred Hunter, and James Boarman jumped guards in Model Industries building, broke through rear window, but were spotted swimming. Boarman fatally wounded; Brest and Hunter picked up by prison launch. Hamilton found hiding in cave.

August 7, 1943—Ted Walters sneaked out of laundry, climbed over fence, but was found entering bay with two large cans tied around waist for buoyancy.

July 31, 1945—John Giles collected entire army uniform over eight years. Stripped off coveralls that concealed uniform and walked onto Army launch. Precautionary count taken on boat revealed extra man.

May 2, 1946—Bernard Coy, Joseph Cretzer, Sam Shockley, Marvin Hubbard, Miran Thompson, and Clarence Carnes—Overpowered guards, captured weapons, took over cellhouse, but did not get key to exterior door. By end of siege, guards William Miller and Harold Stites and convicts Coy, Cretzer, and Hubbard were dead. Shockley and Thompson were executed. Carnes returned to prison.

July 23, 1956—Floyd Wilson disappeared from dock crew and hid in crevice in rocks, eluding search parties for 12 hours before being discovered.

September 29, 1958—Clyde Johnson and Aaron Burgett tied guard to tree and ran from garbage detail to shoreline. Johnson found clinging to sea wall. Thirteen days later Burgett's body discovered in bay.

June 11, 1962—Frank Morris and brothers Clarence and John Anglin escaped from cells through enlarged air vents. Dummy heads left in beds. Men climbed to roof along ventilator shaft, down cast-iron stovepipe, entered water with floatation devices made from raincoats. Were never seen again.

December 4, 1962—Last escape attempt—John Paul Scott and Carl Parker sawed through bars in basement room under kitchen. Using inflated gloves inside clothes for extra buoyancy, they jumped in water. Parker gave up and turned back. Scott found clinging to rocks near Golden Gate Bridge, too exhausted to move.

ESCAPING ALCATRAZ

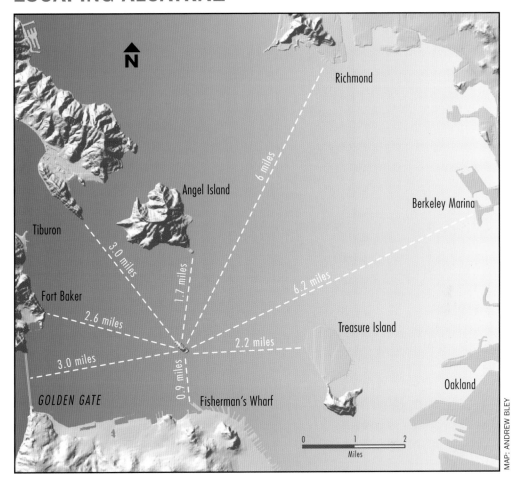

MAP: ANDREW BLEY

With few exceptions, films in which Alcatraz is a focal point involve an escape. In these films, inmates easily slip away from the island, swimming to shore or a nearby lighthouse. As the men who tried it in real life could have testified, the reality was quite different—their elaborate plans were often followed by tragic results.

During the 29 years (1934–1963) that Alcatraz was a federal penitentiary, thirty-four men tried to escape (two tried twice)—seven were shot and killed, one drowned, two were later executed, and five were never found (Ralph Roe and Ted Cole, who disappeared from the industries area in 1937, and Frank Morris and John and Clarence Anglin, in 1962). The other nineteen were returned alive. In stark contrast to almost every previous Alcatraz film—many of which showed convicts deciding to break out of prison, and moments later swimming to shore—*Escape from Alcatraz* was the first to dramatize the laborious planning involved.

MICKEY COHEN
HOLLYWOOD GANGSTER
ALCATRAZ PRISONER

In the 1940s and '50s, Mickey Cohen was the undisputed mob boss of Los Angeles, living an extravagant lifestyle and hobnobbing with movie stars and moguls; he was truly a Hollywood gangster. A fastidious dresser with an elaborate personal hygiene routine, Mickey filled his closets with the most expensive clothes, and drove around in a Cadillac convertible (followed by a "protection" car). His crimes included bookmaking, fixing fights, embezzlement, assault with deadly weapons, conspiracy to obstruct justice, and suspicion of murders (quite a few of his bookmaking rivals ended up murdered, as well as one of his lawyers, who was shot outside of his home).

Meeting Al Capone

Growing up in Los Angeles, Mickey went to New York to become a prizefighter, but ended up using his fists working in the organized crime racket. Mickey went to Chicago, met Al Capone (who, like Mickey, would also get nailed on tax-evasion charges and serve time on Alcatraz), and worked in the gambling racket. "I walked into his office kind of awed, because I was a young kid walking into the office of Al Capone," Mickey said years later. "He did something which was a very big thing for me—he kind of held my head and kissed me on both cheeks."

The Hood in Hollywood

Working with famed gangster Benjamin "Bugsy" Siegel, he formed the West Coast extension of the "Syndicate." Together they built a multimillion-dollar business in gambling and narcotics, supported by their union and political connections. As head of the Syndicate's West Coast operations, Mickey and Siegel began meeting with the movers and shakers of Hollywood. It was known that Mickey did favors for many of Tinsel Town's elite citizens. While Mickey was doing time at McNeil Island on income tax evasion, his friend Johnny Stompanato began dating the rich and glamorous MGM star Lana Turner, who struggled with alcoholism and had a series of famous boyfriends and husbands. In 1958, Turner's only child, Cheryl Crane (then 14 years old), killed Stompanato with a kitchen knife. At the conclusion of her trial, she was found to have committed justifiable homicide and set free. Though Mickey didn't believe that Cheryl killed Johnny, he was public about the trial's outcome: "This is the first time I've ever heard of a guy being convicted of his own murder."

"I didn't kill anyone that didn't deserve killing in the first place."

Mickey Cohen

On Alcatraz

In 1961, Mickey Cohen was convicted of tax evasion and sentenced to Alcatraz. He was 47 years old, stood 5'6", and weighed 165 lbs when he arrived on the Rock. The *San Francisco Examiner* described him as a "socially prominent, ice-cream parlor public relations executive in Los Angeles", and as "a dapper little hoodlum." Shortly after he arrived, Cohen was granted bond (a first for an Alcatraz inmate), and released. He left Alcatraz on October 16, 1961, and according to the SF newspapers, he went straight to the Fairmont Hotel. He booked a room, then got a haircut and a massage. Newspapers said that he had made three trips to the barbershop and took five baths that day. He said of Alcatraz, "I'm not going back. My appeal is solid and I'll win." On Tuesday, May 17, 1962, under a banner headline "Cohen in Chains Back on the Rock", he was photographed stepping onto the *Warden Johnston* headed to Alcatraz.

Cohen described his Alcatraz experiences in his autobiography, *In My Own Words*. As might be expected, he had little good to say about the prison. And, like others before him, his perceptions were no doubt colored by a desire to cast himself as the victim of—rather than a predator on—society and its institutions. "I'll tell you truthfully, if a man went through there for any length of time, he had to be a tremendously strong person to come out of there as a human being," claimed Mickey. He said guards beat up prisoners, and inmates "lived in fear" of other prisoners: "Like if you're walking around a corner, you're liable to get a shiv put in your back." Cohen also told stories of how guards would get him steaks from a local restaurant and deliver them to his cell.

Mickey Cohen's standards of personal hygiene were well known, and the prison had a policy of one shower and one uniform change per week. Luckily, he was assigned to the clothing issue area, which gave him access to showers. As he said in his autobiography, showering "was the only thing that saved my life. It was a godsend to me because I would have probably blown my top if I couldn't bathe." Harvey Keitel played Mickey in the movie *Bugsy* (1991).

1962 ....

BIRDMAN OF ALCATRAZ

Directed by
JOHN FRANKENHEIMER

NORMA PRODUCTIONS / UNITED ARTISTS
147 minutes, Black and White

CAST

Burt Lancaster	Robert Stroud
Karl Malden	Harvey Shoemaker
Thelma Ritter	Elizabeth Stroud
Neville Brand	Bull Ransom
Telly Savalas	Feto Gomez
Betty Field	Stella Johnson
Edmond O'Brien	Tom Gaddis
Hugh Marlowe	Roy Comstock
Whit Bissell	Dr. Ellis

CREATIVE

Executive Producer	Harold Hecht
Producer	Stuart Millar, Guy Trosper
Novel	Thomas E. Gaddis
Screenplay	Guy Trosper
Cinematography	Burnett Guffey
Editing	Edward Mann
Art Direction	Fernando Carrere
Music	Elmer Bernstein

INSIDE THE ROCK CALLED ALCATRAZ THEY TRIED TO CHAIN A VOLCANO THEY CALLED 'THE BIRD MAN'!

HAROLD HECHT PRESENTS
BURT
LANCASTER

BIRD
MAN
OF
ALCATRAZ

co-starring
KARL MALDEN / THELMA RITTER / NEVILLE BRAND

EDMOND O'BRIEN as Tom Gaddis

with BETTY FIELD TELLY SAVALAS

screenplay by GUY TROSPER based on the book by TOM GADDIS

directed by JOHN FRANKENHEIMER

produced by STUART MILLAR and GUY TROSPER

music ELMER BERNSTEIN   A NORMA PRODUCTION   released thru UNITED UA ARTISTS

MP1212

Robert Stroud is sent to federal prison in Leavenworth, Kansas, after being found guilty in Alaska of the murder of Charles Donner, who had beaten up his friend, Katie Malone. Stroud quickly becomes a problem prisoner and his hot temper gets him into a number of skirmishes. Stroud's mother Elizabeth makes the 2,000-mile trip from Alaska to see him, but shows up on a Saturday when visitors are not allowed. When Stroud finds out she was turned away, his anger explodes and he kills a guard. Stroud is sentenced to death for this, his second killing, but Elizabeth manages to convince the country's First Lady to intervene. Stroud's death sentence is commuted, but he must spend the rest of his life in "deep lock," or solitary confinement.

Alone in the recreation yard one day, Stroud finds a fallen sparrow. He takes the bird to his cell, feeds it, nurtures it, and teaches it to fly. Others inmates want birds and get them, but they soon lose interest; Stroud takes their birds, fashioning nests from socks, water bowls from bottles, and painstakingly building birdcages out of wooden boxes. Soon, Stroud's cell is filled with birds and cages. One day, the chirping stops and the birds begin dying. Stroud cleans his cell, sterilizes the cages, and reads medical journals from the prison library. Using chemicals sent to him by his mother, Stroud experiments until he finally discovers a formula that saves his birds. News of his research spreads among bird enthusiasts. When his work wins a contest, the prize is delivered to Stroud in prison by Stella Johnson. Stella and Stroud take an immediate liking to each other, and decide to start a business together: he makes the medicine, and she sells it. Though in confinement, Stroud is able to research the topic of avian illnesses, and after seven years, publishes *Stroud's Digest of the Diseases of Birds*, establishing himself as the world's foremost authority on the subject.

Then, without warning, Stroud is transferred to Alcatraz, where he is not allowed to have birds or research equipment. Stroud begins working on a new book, an exhaustive examination of the prison system (*Looking Outward: An Historic and Analytic Study of the Federal Penal System from the Inside*)—about caged men rather than birds—and what prison does to them. The Alcatraz warden confiscates the manuscript, berates Stroud for his denunciation of the penal system, and suspends all his privileges.

Stroud had been in solitary confinement for four and a half years, when, in 1946, the worst riot in Alcatraz history erupts. The convicts take over the cellhouse, prison guards are killed, inmates are shot, and the prison is ripped apart. Outside, officials stage a huge blockade. Stroud remains in his cell, but when the riot subsides, he takes a gun and throws it out as a peace offering, ending the siege.

Fifteen years later, Stroud leaves Alcatraz when he is transferred to another prison.

ROBERT STROUD IN HOSPITAL CELL, CIRCA 1948, AND CELL TODAY

THE INSIDE SCOOP

In the 1960s, a number of filmmakers were making strong, socially conscious dramas about the harsh realities of life. Like *Birdman*, many were filmed in black-and-white to further emphasize the starkness of these difficult modern-day stories—for example, *The Hustler* (1961), about a gambling obsession; *The Days of Wine and Roses* (1962), about alcoholism; *The Slender Thread* (1965), about suicide; and *Who's Afraid of Virginia Woolf* (1966), about a tumultuous marriage.

The release of *Birdman of Alcatraz* in 1962 marked a distinct change in films about Alcatraz and about prisons in general. Prior to *Birdman*, most filmmakers had taken a hands-off approach to commenting on the penal system, and *Birdman* was among the earliest movies to attack prisons and their lack of rehabilitation. Noteworthy is the exceptional 1954 movie, *Riot in Cellblock 11*, about prisoners who riot in the hopes of changing an abusive prison system. That film's many Alcatraz movie connections include its star Neville Brand, who plays correctional officer Bill Ransom in *Birdman*, director Don Siegel (*Escape from Alcatraz*, 1979), and producer Walter Wanger (*House Across the Bay*, 1940).

Birdman of Alcatraz was the first film to draw upon the history of the island and its inmates; though manipulated and shaded for dramatic effect, the stories of Robert Stroud and the infamous "Battle of 1946" have a basis in fact. When Tom Gaddis's book *Birdman of Alcatraz* was suggested for a movie, it had a difficult time getting made, reportedly due to pressure from the Federal Bureau of Prisons. They didn't want murderer Stroud, who was still in prison, to be turned into a hero in the guise of film star Burt Lancaster. They refused access to Alcatraz for filming *Birdman*, so a costly set was built to replicate the prison. (*Birdman*'s "Alcatraz D Block" was accurate except for one glaring error: there are no windows in these cells.)

101

The movie opens with a shot of Alcatraz and ends with Stroud's transfer from Alcatraz, but very little film time is spent on the island. In fact, Stroud never had birds while incarcerated in Alcatraz, but like many Alcatraz films, Gaddis's bestselling book, *Birdman of Alcatraz*, took advantage of the island's well-known name and reputation. Nearly all of the film takes place in Leavenworth Federal Penitentiary, where convicted murderer Robert Stroud kept and studied birds, but the unique story of the *Birdman*, coupled with the notoriety of Alcatraz, captured the public's attention, and they will forever be indelibly linked.

When a film star of Burt Lancaster's stature decided to take on the role of convict Robert Stroud, the island prison became the focus of a huge Hollywood marketing campaign. The film received four Oscar nominations and numerous other awards. *Birdman*'s difficult subject did not prove to be a big box office draw, but the film played well overseas due to the many silent scenes of Lancaster working with birds. The lack of dialogue eased the language barrier, and, coupled with Lancaster's fame, the movie helped promote Alcatraz Island to an international audience. Released twelve years after the last Alcatraz film (*Experiment Alcatraz*, 1950), the popularity of the film through movie rentals continues to encourage visitors to see Alcatraz, now one of the Golden Gate National Parks. USP Alcatraz closed one year after the release of *Birdman*, but a new chapter in its celluloid identity was just beginning.

the studio: UNITED ARTISTS AND HECHT-HILL-LANCASTER

United Artists was established in 1919 by filmmakers to protect and support artists over management. The studio's primary business was to distribute films, but in the mid-'40s, financial problems ensued, and by 1951, they were forced to make major changes. Arthur Krim and Robert Benjamin took over management, and UA began to play a larger role in financing films and sharing in their profits. This new team sought relationships with many actor-producers, including Executive Producer Howard Hecht and Burt Lancaster. In 1954, as Lancaster's box-office power was exploding, the two men started one of the first independent production companies, Hecht-Lancaster (HL), and produced a series of hits including *Apache* and *Vera Cruz* (both 1954), and *The Kentuckians* (1955). Later, teaming with James Hill (HHL) and working through United Artists, they won the Best Picture Oscar for *Marty* (1955), and released their biggest success, *Trapeze* (1956). As time went on, the company had financial problems, experiencing losses with *The Sweet Smell of Success* (1957), *Run Silent, Run Deep* (1958), and *The Devil's Disciple* (1959), and finally closed down in 1959.

THE REAL ROBERT STROUD

Robert Stroud was a physically aggressive sociopath, who, though often stable, could be dangerous when bored or angry. He was highly intelligent, with an IQ ranging from 150 to 160. Robert Stroud did not have birds on Alcatraz. He gained recognition among bird breeders and prison guards because of his bird studies and books, written while at USP Leavenworth, KS, but his worldwide reknown (he was the most famous prisoner in America) came with the release of the book (by Thomas Gaddis, which was translated into several languages), and the movie *Birdman of Alcatraz*.

Stroud arrived on Alcatraz on December 19, 1942, and spent seventeen years on the island, six and a half years in isolation cell #42, D Block, and eleven years in an Alcatraz hospital cell for both his medical (psychiatric) condition and security concerns. In one of Stroud's comments to his parole board, he gave the reason for wanting his release as "to kill more people." Stroud was very active during the 1946 riot. According to Phil Bergen, who was a guard in the D Block gun gallery, Stroud negotiated with the guards and pleaded with them to stop the bombardment of the isolation block. Stroud was also known to have left his cell at one point to close the heavy doors to the dark cells in order to protect the men locked in them.

According to Alcatraz historian Jolene Babyak, "Lancaster was enlisted to help sell the public on the idea that Stroud needed to be set free." Birdman author Thomas Gaddis and Hollywood real estate lawyer Stanley Furman traveled the country to promote the film and their cause to free Stroud, and it's difficult to say which motivation was greater. The campaign failed, though at seventy-one, after fifty-three years in prison, Stroud was unlikely to ever be released. As Babyak, author of *Birdman, The Many Faces of Robert Stroud*, says, "In fact, both of Robert Stroud's killings were executions. According to the coroner, in Stroud's first killing in 1909, the trajectory of the bullet went from the temple through the abdomen. You have to be standing over someone in order to pull that off. In his second killing in 1916, Stroud raised his hand for permission to speak, got off his bench while eating lunch in Leavenworth federal penitentiary and stabbed the guard near the heart—in front of 1,100 prisoners!"

Robert Stroud died on November 21, 1963, spending his last days at the US Medical Center for Federal Prisoners in Springfield, Missouri. His death went largely unnoticed, eclipsed by the assassination of President John F. Kennedy on November 22, 1963. While in Springfield, Stroud was given a battery of psychological tests and found to, indeed, be a psychopath.

STARRING

BURT LANCASTER's enormous presence dominates every scene in *Birdman of Alcatraz*, and his restrained portrayal (no matter how unlike the real Robert Stroud) earned him an Academy Award nomination and the Best Actor Award at the Venice Film Festival. Lancaster's obsession in making the film shows in the intensity of his performance. He is strident in every action, willful, determined, and angry. Unfortunately, Lancaster's enthusiasm for Stroud's humanity overwhelms the real Robert Stroud's deep psychosis. When Lancaster portrays Stroud, he does so with heroic force, but the complexity of a character like Stroud is diminished when played without seeing the killer inside him. Though we watch Lancaster thrust a knife into a guard, it's presented with bravado and not seen as a psychotic episode. Still, Lancaster is a compelling actor to watch.

Lancaster read everything he could about Stroud and tried, without success, to have first-hand interviews with the prisoner and his family and lawyers. "He put everything on hold, turned down other more lucrative movies, to 'tinker' as Hecht [executive producer] later described it, and groom his very noncommercial project. It was his masterwork, a creation out of the prison of his own self," wrote Kate Buford, author of *Burt Lancaster, An American Life*. Lancaster was the driving force behind the film, working daily, meticulously, and often contentiously with director Frankenheimer to craft *Birdman*.

The subject matter of *Birdman of Alcatraz* was not highly commercial, but Lancaster was at the height of his film career and had tremendous influence on his movies. He had won the Academy Award for *Elmer Gantry* in 1960 (during the making of *Birdman*) and was named number one box-office star in America. Lancaster's films include *The Killers* (1946), *Sorry, Wrong Number* (1948), *Come Back Little Sheba* (1952), *From Here to Eternity* (1953), *The Rose Tattoo* (1955), *The Rainmaker* (1956), *Gunfight at the OK Corral* (1957), *Sweet Smell of Success* (1957), *Separate Tables* (1958), *Judgment at Nuremberg* (1961), and in one of his most acclaimed performances opposite Susan Sarandon in *Atlantic City* (1980), earning a fourth Academy Award nomination.

THELMA RITTER (Elizabeth Stroud) was well known for her comedic, wisecracking, roles in such celebrated films as *All About Eve* (1950), *Rear Window* (1954), and *Pillow Talk* (1959), more than for her tragic roles, which included a heartbreaking performance in the film noir classic, *Pickup on South Street*. Playing the unsympathetic mother of killer Stroud, Ritter delivers a severe, no-nonsense performance, and though small in stature, Ritter is a forceful match to Lancaster's powerful presence, and earned her sixth Oscar nomination as Best Supporting Actress.

NEWS PHOTO TAKEN DURING BATTLE OF '46; NOTE SMOKE FROM GRENADES AND GUARDS AT LEFT

KARL MALDEN's (Harvey Shoemaker) distinctive presence was well suited to his hard-nosed role as Alcatraz's warden, and provided a strong balance to Lancaster. His career included an Oscar in 1951 for A *Streetcar Named Desire*, *On the Waterfront* (1954, Oscar nomination), *Baby Doll* (1956), *The Cincinnati Kid* (1965), and *Patton* (1970). In 1972, at age 60, Malden was back in the Bay Area costarring with Michael Douglas in the TV series, *The Streets of San Francisco*.

TELLY SAVALAS (Feto Gomez) was a newcomer in 1962 when he made *Birdman*, but he stood out as an agitated fellow inmate who befriends Stroud. He brings the only humor to the film's somber tone through his streetwise slang, and his performance earned him a Best Supporting Actor Oscar nomination. Savalas played many psychopaths in films, but found fame in 1973 playing a tough TV detective in *Kojak*.

NEVILLE BRAND (Bull Ransom) was among the most decorated soldiers of WWII. His intelligent but rough looks often led to him being cast as the heavy in movies, but in *Birdman*, he gracefully plays sympathetic guard Bull Ransom, who befriends Stroud. Brand gave a lead performance in the archetypal prison drama *Riot in Cellblock 11*, and portrayed notorious gangster (and Alcatraz prisoner) Al Capone three times, twice in two feature-length *"Untouchable"* TV movies, *The Scarface Mob* (1959) and *Alcatraz Express* (1962), and in the *George Raft Story* (1961).

"No matter what happens to me,
no matter where I am,
if I ever get a chance to punish you further,
I'LL DO IT."

Warden Harvey Shoemaker to inmate Robert Stroud after Stroud kills a guard,
Birdman of Alcatraz

BEHIND THE SCENES

Director JOHN FRANKENHEIMER was not the first director for *Birdman of Alcatraz*. When production started in 1960, Briton Charles Crichton (*The Lavender Hill Mob*, 1951) was at the helm; Crichton lasted only a month, then Lancaster brought in John Frankenheimer. Though the two had worked acrimoniously on their first collaboration, *The Young Savages* (1961), Lancaster knew that he was the right director for *Birdman*. Working closely, often clashing, they shaped *Birdman* into a skillfully textured personal drama about one man's internal struggle. The first cut was over four hours long, and Frankenheimer had to rewrite while Lancaster was making the star-studded *Judgment at Nuremberg* (1961). Lancaster later finished the editing when Frankenheimer left to work on the exceptional political drama, *The Manchurian Candidate* (1962). The confinement of the prison setting brought out the best in Frankenheimer, who was known for his tense, edgy work in the tight sets and small screen of television. He received both a Director's Guild and a Golden Lion nomination for his work. This was the start of a string of significant films for the director, including *Seven Days in May* (1964), *The Train* (1964, with Lancaster), *Seconds* (1966), and *Grand Prix* (1966).

Cinematographer BURNETT GUFFEY is one of the most respected talents in the business, winning two Oscars and three Oscar nominations for his cinematography in *From Here to Eternity* (Oscar 1953, black and white), *The Harder They Fall* (1957), *Birdman* (1963), *King Rat* (1966), and *Bonnie and Clyde* (Oscar 1968, color). *Birdman*'s running time of 147 minutes inside the walls of a prison makes Guffey's black-and-white photography a crucial element of the film's success. Guffey illuminates Stroud's life inside prison, angling his camera and creating layers of depth through the bars and shadows of caged men and birds.

Editor EDWARD MANN does the best work of his career in *Birdman of Alcatraz*, (his most well known film). Mann started his career in 1933 at RKO filming comedy and musical shorts starring the vaudeville team of Clark and McCullough, comedian Edgar Kennedy, and singer Ruth Etting. He made *Larceny on the Air*, his first Republic Picture, in 1937, and worked with the studio for the next five years on Roy Rogers and Gene Autry Westerns. Mann's films include *Dillinger* (1945), *The Chase* (1946), and *Attack of the 50 Foot Woman* (1958).

Screenwriter GUY TROSPER received a Writers Guild nomination for his *Birdman* script, based on the Thomas Gaddis novel. The dialogue, crafted to show Stroud's humanity and the uncaring prison system, was redeemed from its didactic tendencies by the forthrightness of Lancaster's presentation. Trosper died two years after *Birdman*, at the age of 52, but not before he penned the screenplay (with John Le Carré and Paul Dehn) for the gripping espionage film, *The Spy Who Came in From the Cold* (1965).

Novelist THOMAS GADDIS, a writer and educator in the field of correctional systems, is best remembered as the author of *Birdman of Alcatraz: The Story of*

Robert F. Stroud, upon which the film was based. Gaddis also was co-author of *Killer: A Journal of Murder*, and taught criminology and psychology in Oregon. A former probation officer in Los Angeles, CA, Gaddis was founding director of the National Newgate Prison Projects.

Composer ELMER BERNSTEIN was one of Hollywood's great film composers; he scored more two hundred films and was nominated for fourteen Oscars. Bernstein's thoughtful music for *Birdman* echoes the delicacy of Stroud's small birds and his internal struggle with life behind bars. As Stroud's bird studies take off, Bernstein introduces a Western "gallop" (he was particularly known for his work in the Western genre) to express the momentum. His scores include *Man with the Golden Arm* (1955), *The Ten Commandments* (1956), *The Great Escape* (1963), *Thoroughly Modern Mille* (1967, Oscar), *The Grifters* (1990), and *Far From Heaven* (2002). One of Bernstein's most familiar scores (made more famous later when it was used as part of a cigarette commercial) is the rousing and iconic Western theme for *The Magnificent Seven* (1960).

film poster

After WWII and in connection with government's anti-trust investigations, the movie business was forced to modify the lucrative relationships they had previously enjoyed with theaters. This weakened the studios and opened the way for independent filmmakers to become a force in the movie business; no longer as beholden to the studios, directors began to call the shots, including the marketing of their films to create a particular look for their work.

In the 1960s, as this development progressed, there was an explosion in graphic arts led by Andy Warhol, Peter Max, Milton Glaser, and Saul Bass, among others. By the time *Birdman* was made, Bass was a legend in his field, having developed relationships with filmmakers who were influential in the marketing of their work, notably Otto Preminger and Alfred Hitchcock. Though the poster for *Birdman* is often attributed to Bass, who worked with both Burt Lancaster (*Trapeze*, 1956) and John Frankenheimer (*Grand Prix*, 1966), according to family members, Saul Bass did not create the image. However, it was certainly inspired by his work, especially his use of flat color and bold graphics. Regardless of the artist behind the poster, it is an outstanding and memorable movie graphic.

SOLITARY CONFINEMENT, D BLOCK; ARROW POINTS TO ROBERT STROUD'S TOP CORNER CELL

"Don't be afraid. Out there you can kick up the dust, watch
the alfalfa bloom, taste sweet whisky, or red-eyed gravy.
The air breathes easy, nights move faster, and you tell time
by the clock. Now, you don't want to be a jailbird all your life,
do you? You're a highballing sparrow, so you fly high old
cock. Go out there and bite the stars for me."

Robert Stroud speaking to one of his birds, *Birdman of Alcatraz*

POINT BLANK

Directed by
JOHN BOORMAN

MGM
92 minutes, Color

CAST

Lee Marvin	Walker
Angie Dickinson	Chris
Keenan Wynn	Yost
Carroll O'Connor	Brewster
John Vernon	Mal Reese
Lloyd Bochner	Fredrick Carter
Michael Strong	John Stegman
Sharon Acker	Lynne
James Sikking	Hired Gun

CREATIVE

Producer	Judd Bernard, Robert Chartoff
Author (*The Hunter*)	Donald E. Westlake *(as Richard Stark)*
Screenplay	Alexander Jacobs, David Newhouse, Rafe Newhouse
Cinematography	Philip H. Lathrop
Editing	Henry Berman
Art Direction	Albert Brenner, George W. Davis
Original Music	Stu Gardner (song *"Mighty Good Times"*) Johnny Mandel
Set Decoration	F. Keogh Gleason, Henry Grace
Costumes	Margo Weintz *(uncredited)*
Visual Effects	J. McMillan Johnson

Metro-Goldwyn-Mayer presents
A Judd Bernard-Irwin Winkler
Production starring
LEE MARVIN
"POINT BLANK"

There are two kinds of people in his up-tight world:
his victims and his women. And sometimes you can't tell them apart.

co-starring ANGIE DICKINSON

KEENAN WYNN · CARROLL O'CONNOR · LLOYD BOCHNER · MICHAEL STRONG

Screenplay by Alexander Jacobs and David Newhouse & Rafe Newhouse   Based on the novel "The Hunter" by Richard Stark

Directed by John Boorman   Produced by Judd Bernard and Robert Chartoff   **In Panavision and Metrocolor**

 Suggested For Mature Audiences

 MGM

PRINTED IN UK

Small-time hoodlum Walker agrees to help his desperate friend, Mal Reese, steal money to pay off a mob debt. The drop-off is on deserted Alcatraz Island; there, Walker and Reese intercept the delivery, kill two men, and take the money. Walker's wife Lynne is also on the island, and unbeknownst to Walker, Lynne and Reese are having an affair. As Walker reclines in one of the prison's cells, Reese shoots him, then he and Lynne take the money and leave. Walker, however, doesn't die. After regaining consciousness, he makes his way out of the prison to the edge of the island and into the water, where he drifts on the tide back to San Francisco.

Some time later, a recovered Walker and a man named Yost are on a tour boat circling Alcatraz. Yost tells Walker that Reese is now a big shot in the mob (called the "Organization"), and that he used Walker's share of the Alcatraz money to buy his way in. Walker wants the $93,000 he's owed, and Yost makes a deal with him: He'll help Walker get his money if Walker helps him take over the Organization. Walker agrees, and Yost gives him the address where Lynne and Reese are living in Los Angeles.

In LA, Walker finds Lynne, who tells him Reese moved out and their only contact is the money he sends her every week by messenger. That night, Lynne dies after taking an overdose of sleeping pills, but Walker stays at her house, waiting for the delivery. Finding out that it comes from someone named Stegman, he proceeds to track him down, and is told that Reese has been sleeping with Lynne's sister Chris.

Walker finds Chris at home; she tells him that, indeed, Reese wants her, but that she hates him because he killed her lover. She agrees to take Walker to Reese's penthouse apartment and through his considerable security. Once inside, Walker pulls a gun on Reese and demands his money. Reese says he doesn't have it, and that Carter controls the money. The two men fight, and Reese falls over his penthouse balcony to his death. Walker confronts Carter at his downtown LA office, where they arrange to meet later at a money drop in one of LA's cavernous storm drains. However, Carter double-crosses Walker, and pays the price with his life. Next, Yost takes Walker to a swank LA house to meet his next mark, Brewster, Carter's boss, who's expected to return to the house the following morning. When Brewster arrives the next day, Walker asks for his $93,000, but Brewster says he doesn't have it—that they don't deal in cash anymore, that it's all in investments. After Walker shoots at Brewster, he confesses that there's still one set-up left on the Alcatraz Run—which has been moved to Fort Point—and he can get Walker's cash there.

Returning to San Francisco, Walker hides in Fort Point and watches as Brewster retrieves a package of money dropped from a helicopter. Suddenly, a gunshot rings out and Brewster falls to the ground. As he lies dying, he sees Yost and identifies him as Fairfax, the head of the Organization. Fairfax leaves the money for Walker, who disappears into the fort's shadows, never claiming the money he has so arduously pursued.

THE INSIDE SCOOP

In 1967, *Point Blank* was largely ignored by the public and disregarded by many critics, but it's now considered one of the best movies of the 1960s. Based on Donald Westlake's novel, *The Hunter*, about white-collar organized crime in modern America, *Point Blank*'s 34-year-old British director John Boorman broke the mold of gangster and noir films and helped kick off the American neo-noir movement. "There was a kind of explosiveness in filmmaking," said Boorman, who was influenced by the British and French New Wave and Italian masters Fellini and Anotonioni. *Point Blank*, however, is distinctly American, especially in its fascination with violence. Along with *Bonnie and Clyde* (1967) and *Bullitt* (1968), it introduced a bold viewpoint on violence in films and set the stage for the '70s explosion of this genre, including Don Siegel's *Dirty Harry* (1971) series (see *The Enforcer*).

THE NOIR GANGSTER REINVENTED

In this, his second film (his first was the heralded *Catch Me If You Can*, 1965, with the Dave Clark Five), Boorman pares down a revenge story and transforms it into a dynamic study of one gangster's journey toward retribution. Boorman's visual storytelling techniques are stunning. In reinventing the noir picture, he discards its tight sets and shadowy darks and lights, and instead films in widescreen Panavision, using bright LA daylight, dramatic color palettes, and provocative editing. Instead of elaborate dialogue-driven storylines, Boorman experiments with the non-linear narrative, employing flashbacks, repetitive action, soft-focus shots, screens, and slow-motion scenes to reveal Walker's shattered memories.

For example, in one sequence, Walker strides resolutely down a long, stark airport corridor. This is intercut with scenes of his deceitful wife Lynne getting up, putting on make-up, dressing, going out, and returning home. Throughout, we hear only the pounding beat of Walker's steps. The two collide when Marvin explodes into the house brandishing a gun, grabs his wife, and shoots at an empty bed with a Smith & Wesson .44 Magnum (the same gun Clint Eastwood would later make famous in *Dirty Harry*). It's a riveting sequence, and like many others, is presented completely without dialogue.

Color is a key element in the film, and Boorman employs it to convey a mysterious sense of unreality. According to Boorman, by using monochromatic color schemes he was able to give the effect of the film noir style. Supervised by William Stair, the movie moves from cold to warm, starting with the hard cement and fencing of Alcatraz and leading us into Lynn's sleek mirrored house (both Lynn and Walker wear muted gray). When Angie Dickinson's character is introduced, the colors change to yellows and golds. The corporate office of the mob, or Organization as it's called, is presented in a spectrum of greens—couch, walls, chairs, and even these modern gangsters' suits and ties display a verdant tone. The film moves to the brown wood paneling in an upscale LA home before finally ending in the magnificent red brick masonry of Fort Point.

Point Blank presents the gangster as a modern-day executive in corporate America. The Organization functions like any big business, with headquarters in sleek LA towers and bosses in prime corner-office locations. Executives wear suits and ties, carry briefcases, and live in penthouse apartments. Maintaining a streamlined operation, they fly private jets, no longer deal in cash (investments only), and hire sharpshooters to handle problems. Originally, the film was set entirely in San Francisco, but after visiting the city, Boorman felt it to be too "pastel and pleasant", and moved the central part of the story to the harsh, spread-out landscape of Los Angeles.

DEAD OR ALIVE

From the beginning, *Point Blank* leads us to question whether Walker is alive or dead (or at least, dying). This ambiguity underlies the film and gives it a sense of mystery. The film opens with a loud gunshot and the sight of Walker lying in an Alcatraz cell. During the opening credits, Walker "rises from the dead," slowly makes his way to the edge of the island and into the water, and then drifts toward San Francisco. Is Walker dead? Is the film Walker's dying dream, an impulse toward resolution?

Boorman introduces many elements that suggest this premise. Walker's "escape from Alcatraz" is put into immediate question when, after being shot, he appears fully recovered on a tourist boat circling the island as an announcer explains the near-impossibility of escaping. Throughout the film, the character of Yost appears ghostlike, out of nowhere, to help Walker find his next "mark." The two men are always alone and never look at each other when they speak. At one point, the furniture in the Lynn's apartment suddenly disappears, and Walker crouches in a corner by two barren windows that look like they have bars on them, evoking the prison on Alcatraz and once again raising the question in the viewer's mind: Did Walker leave the cell where he was shot? In a telling moment, a pissed-off Angie Dickinson tells the emotionless Walker, "You died on Alcatraz, all right." Finally, having achieved his retribution, Walker disappears into the shadows of Fort Point, never claiming the money he has relentlessly pursued.

the studio: **MGM**

Financed and distributed by MGM, *Point Blank* was made as the old Hollywood studio system was waning. The film benefited from an outstanding crew of veteran artists behind the scenes who had learned their craft during the studio's remarkable reign. MGM's fortunes continued to fluctuate through the '60s, but in 1967, when *Point Blank* was released, MGM recorded its top profit at $14 million, thanks to *Dr. Zhivago*, and another Lee Marvin release, *The Dirty Dozen*.

DOCUMENTING THE ROCK

MGM produced two quirky but fascinating documentary shorts in conjunction with *Point Blank*, both of which are titled "The Rock" and appear on the recently released DVD version of the movie. Allowed to actually film on the island and in the cellhouse, the filmmakers understood the unique opportunity they had been given, and the shorts provide the audience with the world's first tour inside the prison. We see behind-the-scenes footage of the filmmaking process and are taken on a personal tour by Angie Dickinson, who gives her own take on Alcatraz: "As I walk through the halls and look into each cell, I can't think of anything that I would want bad enough—no woman, no man, no hatred could be worth this."

The complexity of filming on Alcatraz started with getting all 125 cast and crewmembers onto the island, along with thousands of tons of equipment, which had to be lifted from a barge to the dock by a huge crane. Garnering attention for being the first movie allowed to film on the island, *Point Blank* brought Alcatraz back into the headlines, including an exclusive *Life* magazine fashion shoot with Angie Dickinson wearing the latest '60s fashions.

Alcatraz prisoner (#250), JOHN GILES

In a remarkable slice of historical documentation, the filmmakers brought former Alcatraz prisoner and attempted escapee John Giles to the island. Giles, 77 at the time, speaks solemnly about the infamous 1946 riot and his life while on Alcatraz. "Everything looks just like it did in those days," Giles says upon entering the prison. "Everything was so strict. A man with a long time, he's got only one thought—he wants to escape, needs to escape. You think it's the end of your life. You don't want to die in prison. You have that obsession. That's all you think about. It fills your waking hours from morning to night."

John Giles arrived on Alcatraz on August 28, 1935, a little more than a year after it opened as a federal penitentiary. A long career as a burglar and bank robber (he also had one death to his credit, that of a deputy who was attempting to arrest him), had already provided him with plenty of prison time. He was first convicted and sent to prison in 1915 when he was 20 years old, and over the course of the next twenty years, was in and out of prisons, usually following a successful escape. His ability to slip away from incarceration was, in fact, one of the reasons he was sent to Alcatraz from McNeil Island. While on Alcatraz, he developed a reputation as a quiet, industrious worker. During the several years he worked at the dock area, he secretly stole more than forty items from Alcatraz's military laundry service. On July 31, 1945, after taking off the coveralls that concealed the army uniform he wore beneath, he walked onto an army launch docked at Alcatraz expecting that the next stop was San Francisco and freedom. Unfortunately for Giles, the next stop was nearby Angel Island, and when precautionary counts taken on the boat revealed an extra man, Giles was identified and apprehended. Correctional officers from Alcatraz came to Angel Island and took him back into custody the same day.

ALCATRAZ: REEL TO REAL

Released on August 30, 1967, four years after the federal penitentiary on Alcatraz closed, *Point Blank* is the first Hollywood movie actually filmed on Alcatraz Island. In an interview given by producer Judd Bernard, he tells how this came about: "We wanted to shoot at Alcatraz. I called Jack Valenti [head of the MPAA], an advisor to President Lyndon Johnson. I got a call from my secretary at MGM with a number to call Jack. I dial. A man answers and says, 'Who's this?' I said my name and asked, 'Who's this?' And the man said, 'Lyndon Johnson.' It was a private phone at the White House."

On March 21, 1963, after the final twenty-seven Alcatraz prisoners were transferred, the island became a surplus federal property managed by the General Services Administration. It was under GSA jurisdiction during 1967 when *Point Blank* was filmed, and remained so until 1972, when it was transferred to the Department of the Interior and administered by the National Park Service. *Point Blank* was the only film made on the island before the Indian Occupation (1969–71) that dramatically changed the island's architectural elements. Also, since visiting the island wasn't allowed, the filmmakers had a much easier time getting the location footage they needed.

VIEW OF GUARD TOWER, EASTERN SIDE OF ISLAND

STARRING

LEE MARVIN (Walker) is sensational as the film's protagonist Walker, charging stoically through scenes as he penetrates each level of the organization, determined to get his money. He dominates the film both physically and in his carefully understated performance. Marvin's stature, white hair, and carved-in-stone features reflect the imposing, modern Los Angeles high-rises he stalks, and give him the appearance of invincibility. According to Boorman, Marvin was instrumental to the film's success. In a highly unusual move for Hollywood, Marvin, who had "final cut" of the film, transferred all control to Boorman. Boorman acknowledges that Marvin was not just open to his ideas, but contributed many of his own, helping to realize the film's striking vision.

Marvin's film career took off after playing memorable villains in *The Big Heat* (throwing scalding coffee at Gloria Grahame's face) and *The Wild One* (both 1953). He was in *The Caine Mutiny* (1954, directed by Edward Dmytryk, *Seven Miles from Alcatraz*); challenged Spencer Tracy in *Bad Day at Black Rock* (1955); and played the heavy in many other films. From 1957 to 1960, Marvin starred as Lt. Frank Ballinger in the successful television crime drama *M Squad*. He returned to films opposite John Wayne in Michael Curtiz's last film, *The Comancheros* (1961) and made a string of successful films, including *The Man Who Shot Liberty Valance* (1962), *Donovan's Reef* (1963), and *The Killers* (1964), before striking gold by winning a Best Actor Oscar for his role as twin brothers in *Cat Ballou* (1965). He followed with *Ship of Fools* (1965), *The Professionals* (1966), and *The Dirty Dozen* (1967). After making *Point Blank*, Marvin starred in *Hell in the Pacific* (1968, John Boorman), *Paint Your Wagon* (1969, with Clint Eastwood), *The Big Red One* (1980), and his last film, *The Delta Force* (1986).

After Marvin died, his widow visited Alcatraz and was interviewed by one of the National Park Service rangers. According to Mrs. Marvin, *Point Blank* was her husband's favorite film.

ANGIE DICKINSON's (Chris) stylish looks and vulnerable sensuality, which were a match for Marvin's arrogant cool, were put to particularly effective use in a scene where she attempts to beat up Marvin, uselessly pounding her statue-like costar with her fists and pocketbook until she drops to the floor in exhaustion. Dickinson plays the scene with a zest supposedly inspired by her dislike of Marvin from an earlier film, *The Killers* (1964), during which Marvin hung her out a window.

Dickinson started her film career with Warner Brothers and had small but significant parts in a number of Westerns before being cast opposite Gene Barry in Samuel Fuller's *China Gate* (1957). Her big break came as the female lead in Howard Hawks classic, *Rio Bravo* (1959). Dickinson joined the Rat Pack for the box-office smash *Oceans Eleven* (1960), and in 1961, Warner Brothers released *The Sins*

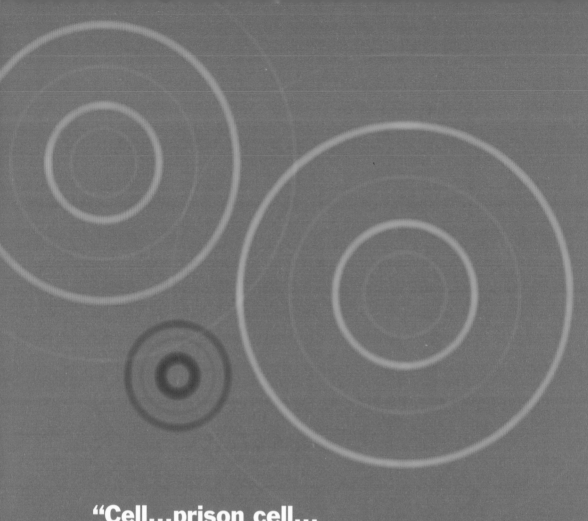

**"Cell...prison cell...
how did I get here?"**

Walker, *Point Blank*

of Rachael Cade, with Dickinson top-billed. She played opposite Marvin in Don Siegel's *The Killers* (1964), opposite Gregory Peck in *Captain Newman, M.D.* (1963), and as Marlon Brando's wife in *The Chase* (1966). Dickinson earned four Emmy nominations for the hit series *Police Woman* (1974–1978), the first female-led television cop show (Don "Red" Barry, star of *Train to Alcatraz*, 1948, appeared in six *Police Woman* episodes). Dickinson's films include *Dressed to Kill* (1980), *Sabrina* (1995), and *Pay It Forward* (2000).

KEENAN WYNN (Yost) was one of Hollywood's most versatile and dependable character actors. Over four decades, he appeared in more than one hundred seventy-five films and television shows. Wynn joined MGM in the early '40s, and appeared in *The Clock* (1945), *Easy to Wed* (1946), *The Hucksters* (1947), and *Kiss Me Kate* (1953). In 1957 he starred with his father, comedian Ed Wynn, Michael Caine, and Sean Connery in the original 1956 teleplay of *Requiem for a Heavyweight*. Wynn's later films include *The Absent-Minded Professor* (1961), *Dr. Strangelove...* (1964), *The Great Race* (1965), and *Nashville* (1975).

JOHN VERNON (Mal Reese) made his US screen debut in *Point Blank*. A classically trained Canadian actor, Vernon appeared in over one hundred films and television shows, often cast as a villain, a corrupt official, or a tough mobster. Vernon's early films include *Topaz* (1969), *Dirty Harry* (1971), *The Outlaw Josey Wales* (1976), and *Brannigan* (1975). In 1978, Vernon was cast in the comedy hit *Animal House*, which began a string of comedic performances.

LLOYD BOCHNER (Carter) is a popular character actor who has appeared in more than one hundred and fifty television shows. As in *Point Blank*, Bochner's suave looks often led to his playing dubious parts as criminals and rich, corrupt businessmen. His films include *The Night Walker* (1964), *Tony Rome* (1967), *Ulzana's Raid* (1972), *The Man in the Glass Booth* (1975), and *Naked Gun 2: The Smell of Fear* (1991). Bochner starred in one of the most popular *Twilight Zone* episodes of all time, *"To Serve Man"* (1959).

CARROLL O'CONNOR (Brewster) will forever be remembered as the exasperatingly narrow-minded Archie Bunker in the groundbreaking television series *All in the Family* (1971–1979), as well as his starring role in the television version of *In the Heat of the Night* (1988–1996). O'Connor's film career was largely made up of supporting parts in *By Love Possessed* (1961), *Lonely Are the Brave* (1962), *Cleopatra* (1963), *In Harm's Way* (1965), *Hawaii* (1966), and *Kelly's Heroes* (1970).

SHARON ACKER (Lynne) gives a touching performance as Walker's cheating wife. Acker has appeared in numerous television shows including *Star Trek* (1969), *Mission Impossible* (1972), *The Streets of San Francisco* (1975), and *Murder She Wrote* (1986), and played Della Street in *The New Perry Mason* (1973–1974).

BEHIND THE SCENES

Director John Boorman is a celebrated filmmaker who gambles on big ideas; *Point Blank*, only his second feature film, is considered by many to be his best. With *Point Blank*, Boorman's re-imagining of the film noir genre influenced future directors, including filmmakers Quentin Tarantino and Steven Soderbergh. Boorman scored a critical and commercial hit with his 1972 film *Deliverance*, about four white-collar friends vacationing on the Appalachian Trail, with disastrous results. Made five years after *Point Blank*, *Deliverance* received Oscar nominations for Best Picture, Director, and Editor, sending Boorman to the top of his field. He followed with the unusual science fiction film *Zardoz* (1974), starring Sean Connery, and *Excalibur* (1981), a stunning retelling of the King Arthur legend. He wrote, produced, and directed *Hope and Glory* (1987), a semi-autobiographical story about a young boy growing up in London during WWII. It received numerous awards, including five Oscar nominations, three for Boorman (Picture, Director, and Screenplay). His other films include *Beyond Rangoon* (1995), *The General* (1998), *The Tailor of Panama* (2001), and *Country of My Skull* (2004).

Cinematographer Philip H. Lathrop created a dazzling look for *Point Blank*. Working with Boorman's color-coded scenes, LA's striking 1960s landscape, and the iconic landmarks of Alcatraz and Fort Point, Lathrop handsomely realized the film's unique vision. He began working in Hollywood in the 1930s, becoming a lighting cameraman in 1957. His first film as cinematographer was on the Universal release *Live Fast, Die Young* (1958). Regarded as an exceptional craftsman, Lathrop's work can be seen in *The Days of Wine and Roses* (1962), *The Americanization of Emily* (1964, Oscar nomination), *They Shoot Horses, Don't They?* (1969), *Earthquake* (1974, Oscar nomination), and *The Killer Elite* (1975). His award-winning television work includes *Malice in Wonderland* (1985), *Christmas Snow* (1986), and *Little Girl Lost* (1988). In 1987, Lathrop was the cinematographer on the television film *Six Against the Rock*, an account of the infamous 1946 Alcatraz escape attempt.

Editor Henry Berman started his career at 19, working for RKO as assistant editor on *Son of Kong* (1933). Nine years the junior of his famed brother, producer Sandro S. Berman, Henry followed in his footsteps and between 1936 and 1942, he edited some of RKO's top films, often working with leading director George Stevens. These films included Rogers and Astaire's *Follow the Fleet* and *Swing Time* (both 1936), *Quality Street* (1937, starring Katherine Hepburn), and *Gunga Din* (1939). His later work includes *Sweet Bird of Youth* (1962) and *Grand Prix* (Oscar, 1966). In 1970 he began a career in television, winning an Emmy for editing *Babe* (1975).

Novelist Donald E. Westlake (*The Hunter*, as Richard Stark) is the prolific author of more than fifty crime and police story novels and screenplays. Westlake began writing mysteries for pulp magazines in the '50s, and novels in the '60s under the name Richard Stark. *The Hunter*, upon which *Point Blank* was based, was the first in a series featuring a tough career criminal, Parker, renamed Walker for the movie. His work includes *The Hot Rock* (1972, novel), *The Stepfather* (1987, story and screenplay), *The Grifters* (1990, screenplay), *Payback* (1999, another remake based on his novel, *The Hunter*), and *Mr. Ripley Returns* (2004, screenplay).

Screenwriters DAVID NEWHOUSE, RAFE NEWHOUSE, and **ALEXANDER JACOBS** crafted a taut, dark script for *Point Blank*. Jacobs wrote the action pictures *Hell in the Pacific* (1968, directed by Boorman and starring Marvin), *The Seven-Ups* (1973), *French Connection II* (1975), and *Enemy of the People* (1978). The stilted dialogue for *Point Blank* is often ambiguous, and enhances the sense of the character's isolation.

Art directors ALBERT BRENNER and **GEORGE W. DAVIS** and **Set decorators F. KEOGH GLEASON** and **HENRY GRACE** are veteran Hollywood artists whose talents on *Point Blank* helped create the film's extraordinary look. Combined, the four men have thirty-eight Oscar nominations and seven statues. Brenner's work includes *Summer of '42* (1971), *The Turning Point* (1977), *2010* (1984), and *Beaches* (1989). Davis's films includes *All About Eve* (1950), *The Robe* (1953), *Funny Face* (1957), and *Diary of Anne Frank* (1959). Gleason's include *An American in Paris* (1951), *The Bad and the Beautiful* (1954), and *Lust for Life* (1957). Grace was the set decorator on *Camille* (1936), *Gigi* (1958), and *North by Northwest* (1959).

Composer JOHNNY MANDEL is a celebrated songwriter and arranger, known for his romantic songs and scores, including *The Shadow of Your Smile* (from *The Sandpiper*, 1965), and music for *M*A*S*H* (1970). Mandel's score for *Point Blank* is something entirely different. Mandel considers himself first and foremost a jazz musician. His provocative work on *Point Blank*, in which the music's eerie texture underlies the tense action, echoes the strained relationships between Walker and the people he encounters.

film poster

The provocative poster for *Point Blank* captures the film's sexual and violent storyline. Pop art exploded in the 1960s and the movement's graphic sensibilities influenced many aspects of American culture, including design, fashion, home decor, and movie posters. Point Blank's poster reflects the era's prevailing visual sensibilities. The use of flat color, concentric circles, and cutout images create an arresting design, and the sexual content of the film is revealed in the provocative photograph of Angie Dickinson lying by her name (the film is known for her brief nude scene). In fact, other posters produced for *Point Blank* are printed with a warning label that states, "Suitable Only for Adults," which reflects not only Dickinson's noticeable assets, but the film's considerable violence.

SKIDOO

Directed by
OTTO PREMINGER

PARAMOUNT PICTURES
97 minutes, Color

CAST

Jackie Gleason	Tony Banks
Carol Channing	Flo Banks
Frankie Avalon	Angie
Fred Clark	Tower Guard
Michael Constantine	Leech
Frank Gorshin	Man
John Phillip Law	Stash
Peter Lawford	The Senator
Burgess Meredith	Alcatraz Warden
George Raft	Captain Garbaldo
Cesar Romero	Hechy
Mickey Rooney	Blue Chips Packard
Groucho Marx	God
Austin Pendleton	Fred the Professor
Alexandra Hay	Darlene Banks
Doro Merande	Mayor
Harry Nilsson	Tower Guard
Slim Pickens	Alcatraz Switchboard Operator

CREATIVE

Producer/Director	Otto Preminger
Screenplay	Doran William Cannon
Cinematography	Leon Shamroy
Editing	George R. Rohrs
Art Direction	Robert Emmet Smith
Music	Harry Nilsson
Set Decoration	Fred Price
Costume Design	Rudi Gernreich
Makeup	Web Overlander, Vivian Thompson

OTTO PREMINGER *presents* "SKIDOO"
starring JACKIE GLEASON · CAROL CHANNING
FRANKIE AVALON · FRED CLARK
MICHAEL CONSTANTINE · FRANK GORSHIN
JOHN PHILLIP LAW · PETER LAWFORD
BURGESS MEREDITH · GEORGE RAFT
CESAR ROMERO · MICKEY ROONEY
and GROUCHO MARX *playing "God"*

and introducing AUSTIN PENDLETON · ALEXANDRA HAY
and LUNA · Written by DORAN WILLIAM CANNON
Music & Lyrics by NILSSON
Costumes RUDI GERNREICH
Photographed in PANAVISION® and
TECHNICOLOR® by LEON SHAMROY
Produced & Directed by OTTO PREMINGER

A Paramount
Release

M Suggested for MATURE audiences
(parental discretion advised).

THE STORY

One night, while retired gangster Tony Banks is at home with his wife Flo and pal Harry, a former underworld associate, Hechy, and his young protégé, Angie, show up. They want Tony to kill Blue Chips Packard, who is sequestered in maximum security at Rock Island Federal Penitentiary (Alcatraz). Packard is about to turn state's evidence against God, Tony's former mob boss. Tony refuses at first, but after finding his pal Harry dead, agrees to do the job.

Tony and Flo's twenty-year old daughter Darlene has a new "hippie" boyfriend, Stash. Stash is introducing Darlene to his hippie friends in a VW bus when the police arrive, arrest everyone, and take them to the Mayor's office. The Mayor is hosting a special committee to clean up ugliness, and wants the hippies thrown out of town, "We don't need you and we don't want you," she says emphatically. Flo is on the committee, and when she sees Darlene, she secretly invites all the hippies to her house. Flo and Darlene get a call from Angie about Tony working for God, and they rush off to his apartment to find out what happened. At first Angie resists, but he falls for Darlene and tells them that only God knows where Tony is. Darlene insists that Angie take them to see God, who lives in a sterile cabin on a yacht off the coast in international waters. Pretty Darlene flirts with God and finds out that Tony is in prison.

Meanwhile, Tony manages to get into Rock Island Federal Penitentiary, where he meets his cellmates, Leech and Fred the Professor, a drug-peddling con. Tony finds out that Packard is in a heavily guarded luxury cell, waiting to testify against God. He knows he's supposed to kill Packard, but after accidentally taking some of the Professor's LSD, realizes two things: He cannot kill Packard, and he must get out of prison. Tony, Leech, and the Professor plan an escape. First, they concoct a temporary "Lithuanian measles" epidemic that sends all three to the infirmary. Next, they spike the water supply with LSD, sending the entire prison population— prisoners and guards alike—on a massive LSD trip. As the prison reverberates with a big, hallucinatory musical number, the cellmates hide in garbage cans, then assemble a hot air balloon from articles found in the prison laundry. As their balloon ascends, God's henchmen shoot at them from his yacht. Coming to the rescue, Flo leads Stash and his hippie friends onto the yacht, just in time for Flo to sing the title song, *Skidoo*, praising flower power.

Tony is saved, a big party follows, and God and the Professor (dressed as Hare Krishnas) sail off in a lifeboat together, smoking pumpkin seeds.

THE INSIDE SCOOP

Skidoo is remembered as Otto Preminger's infamous LSD bomb. Preminger made two decisions that, in retrospect, doomed the movie: he started with a bizarre Alcatraz story by an eccentric writer, Doran William Cannon, and though he cast well-known comedians and celebrities, they were mostly older stars who lacked a connection to the '60s youth culture. The film is filled with scenes that are entertaining only because they're so wacky. Most outrageous are the two musical numbers. The first features garbage cans with arms and legs, singing and dancing about equality inside a can. The second peculiar number features Carol Channing in a long white wig, wearing a mini-skirted red, white, and blue Horatio Hornblower outfit. The combination of Channing's sheer musical force and Nilsson's carefree peace-and-love lyrics is eccentric to say the least. (Supposedly, Preminger took LSD while making the film to understand the effects of the drug. What a strange trip it must have been.) To top it off, the film ends with Harry Nilsson singing all the credits (the first and last time this has ever been done, for obvious reasons). Some good may be said to have come from the film, however. Sixties icon and peace activist Wavy Gravy and his friends had parts in the hippie scenes of *Skidoo*, and used the money they made to purchase buses and present their free "Hog Farm and Friends in Open Celebration" show across the country.

DINING HALL, CIRCA 1950S, AND TODAY

the studio: PARAMOUNT

In 1966, two years before Skidoo was released, Paramount Studios was taken over by a large industrial conglomerate, Gulf +Western Industries. The world was changing radically—Americans were fighting in Vietnam, and a younger generation, experimenting with drugs, sex, and electric guitars, was challenging the establishment. Gulf + Western hired a new young vice-president, actor and producer Robert Evans, as head of production at Paramount. Evans became representative of the "new Hollywood" executive and was able direct Paramount back into Hollywood's biggest studio, producing hit films including *Rosemary's Baby* and *Romeo and Juliet* (both 1968), *The Godfather I* and *II* (1972 and 1974 respectively), *Saturday Night Fever* (1977), and *Grease* (1978). Sigma, a small production company that was behind a number of Otto Preminger films, also produced *Skidoo*.

ALCATRAZ: REEL TO REAL

The film's central story portrays Alcatraz as a fun-loving, drug-ridden, party prison. In 1968, when Skidoo was released, there was no active island prison in San Francisco Bay, as US Penitentiary Alcatraz had ceased to operate in 1963. Skidoo took liberties with the island's reputation, creating a film of pure comedic fantasy unconnected to the real penitentiary, or even to reality in general.

Though the federal penitentiary was closed, no filming was allowed on the island, and Alcatraz is never mentioned by name. The General Services Administration, who had oversight of the island, would not grant Preminger permission to film there, and the FBI also took an interest because an FBI building was included in one of the scenes. The Bureau threatened to prosecute if its name wasn't removed, but didn't follow through (to see FBI documents, visit *www.thesmokinggun.com/skidoo1.html*). To get around this problem, exterior shots establishing the location were taken from a boat. When Gleason is transported to the island, he's actually filmed on a ferry moving toward the real Alcatraz. Late in the film, when Gleason and his cohorts lift off Alcatraz in a hot-air balloon, they do so from a barge anchored behind the island. The camera was mounted on a boat in front of the island, and when the balloon ascends, it seems as though it's launching directly from Alcatraz.

Though *Skidoo*'s inmates are attired in traditional stripes, in fact, prisoners never wore striped uniforms while serving time in USP Alcatraz. In his previous post as warden at San Quentin (a California state prison), James A. Johnston had developed a solid-color uniform, which he put into use at Alcatraz when he became the new prison's first warden in 1934.

Though two men shared a cell in *Seven Miles to Alcatraz* (1942), *Skidoo* went one further, and has Jackie Gleason's character share a cell with two other inmates. In fact, all inmates on Alcatraz had their own cells.

STARRING

JACKIE GLEASON (Tony Banks), known as "The Great One," was a household name when he agreed to join the cast of *Skidoo*, thanks to his two hit television series, *The Honeymooners* (1955–1956) and *The Jackie Gleason Show* (1966–1970). Gleason began his film career at Warner Brothers, but left to find fame on the small screen. He returned to film in 1961 in a dramatic performance as pool shark "Minnesota Fats" in *The Hustler*, which earned him an Oscar nomination. Gleason's film career continued with comedic performances in *Papa's Delicate Condition* (1963), *Don't Drink the Water* (1969), *Smokey and the Bandit* (1977), and *Nothing in Common* (1986). Gleason's role in *Skidoo* is that of an exasperated straight man, and his comedic capacity is lost, subsumed in the rest of the cast's antics. The comedian in him shines through for a brief moment—when his character Tony is in prison, takes LSD, and tries to catch a fly—but sadly, it's a short trip and he reverts to his character's dull persona for the rest of the film.

CAROL CHANNING (Flo Banks) made her name on Broadway, starring in *Gentleman Prefer Blondes* (1949) and *Hello Dolly* (1964). She had appeared in only six motion pictures (with one Oscar nomination for her role in *Thoroughly Modern Millie*, 1967), when she popped up from Frankie Avalon's round hydraulic bed in a yellow bra and panties, an unusual sight even in this film. Channing's outrageous personality is given full reign in this movie, and her enthusiastic rendition of the title song as she dances on a boat mercifully ends the film.

GROUCHO MARX (God) and his brothers, Chico and Harpo, were among the greatest comedians of the 20th century. Their films include *The Coconuts* (1929, by *King of Alcatraz* director Robert Florey), *Monkey Business* (1931), *Horse Feathers* (1932), *Duck Soup* (1933), *A Night at the Opera* (1935), *A Day at the Races* (1937), *Go West* (1940), and *Copacabana* (1947). Groucho moved to television, and hosted a successful quiz show, *You Bet Your Life* (1950–1961). *Skidoo* was, unfortunately, Groucho's last film and he sleepwalks through the entire misadventure.

AUSTIN PENDLETON (The Professor) made his film debut in *Skidoo*. Where most of the cast seems lost, Pendleton is right on the mark, giving a high-strung performance that fits right in with the bizarre story. An accomplished director and actor, Pendleton's acting career ranges from comedic performance in *What's Up Doc* (1971), *Starting Over* (1979), *Guarding Tess* (1994), and *Finding Nemo* (2003, voice of "Gurgle"), to the dramatic *Ballad of a Sad Café* (1991) and *A Beautiful Mind* (2002).

GEORGE RAFT (Captain Garbaldo) and **BURGESS MEREDITH** (Alcatraz Warden) appear in small roles in *Skidoo*. Coincidentally, these two Hollywood stars had leading roles in early Alcatraz films: Raft in *House Across the Bay* (1940), and Meredith in *San Francisco Docks* (1941).

ALCATRAZ ISLAND, SOUTHERN VIEW FROM WATER

BEHIND THE SCENES

Director OTTO PREMINGER was a legendary filmmaker known for many powerful and intriguing movies. Preminger started his movie career under the distrustful eye of Daryl F. Zanuck at 20th Century Fox, until he directed one of the decade's best films, *Laura* (1944), and was given a contract with the studio. Preminger made the strong "woman's" picture, *Daisy Kenyon* (1947) with Joan Crawford, and a number of unexceptional costume stories before directing the sharp thrillers, *Whirlpool* (1949) and *The 13th Letter* (1951). When his contract with Fox expired, he worked independently and made his most ambitious films, including film noir classics *Fallen Angel* (1945) and *Angel Face* (1952); musicals *Carmen Jones* (1954) and *Porgy and Bess* (1959); *Man with the Golden Arm* (1955); the acclaimed courtroom mystery, *Anatomy of a Murder* (1959); the epic *Exodus* (1960); *Advise and Consent* (1962); *The Cardinal* (1963); and *In Harm's Way* (1965). Preminger's films of the late '60s and early '70s were weak, but nothing compares to *Skidoo*, which is an unmitigated disaster. According to an Alcatraz staff member, Preminger's adopted son, who worked on *Skidoo*, said the film was made to meet a contractual agreement.

Screenwriter DORAN WILLIAM CANNON wrote five movies, each with a unique perspective. His most famous film was *Brewster McCloud* (1970), successfully directed by Robert Altman, a strange tale about a young man (Bud Cort) who wants

"Please keep in mind that this penitentiary has been re-equipped with the most modern electronic video and audio devices in order to assist you in paying your debt to society."

Inmate processing instruction, *Skidoo*

to fly using homemade wings inside the Houston Astrodome. He also wrote the 1993 book, *Authorship: The Dynamic Principles of Writing Creatively*.

Singer/songwriter HARRY NILSSON wrote the score for *Skidoo*, as well as singing the closing credits. The whimsical music is as strange as the film, though Nilsson's soothing voice is a pleasant distraction from the mayhem on screen. Nilsson, who also had a small role as one of the prison guards, scored movies and television shows, recorded hit albums, and had a long association with the Beatles. His haunting rendition of Fred Neil's *Everybody's Talking* in the celebrated film *Midnight Cowboy* (1969) won him a Grammy for Best Male Vocalist.

Cinematographer LEON SHAMROY's innovative lighting and camera work brought him early recognition for his handsome black-and-white '30s-era films, and his reputation grew as he moved to color in the '40s and beyond. Shamroy was the force behind 20th Century Fox's outstanding production quality on films such as *The Black Swan* (1942), *Leave Her to Heaven* (1946), *The Snows of Kilimanjaro* (1952), *The King and I* (1956), *South Pacific* (1958), *Cleopatra* (1963), and *The Agony and the Ecstasy* (1965). He received eighteen Oscar nominations and won four times. Shamroy worked with Otto Preminger on seven films; *Skidoo* was his next-to-last picture. His last, *Claudine* (1969) for George Cukor, was another misfire by a celebrated director, but not nearly on the scale of *Skidoo*.

Costume Designer RUDI GERNREICH was a maverick clothes designer of the '50s, '60s, and '70s. Although he only made a few films, his fashion work was revolutionary, changing the way women wore clothes and the amount of skin they were willing to bare. Gernreich has numerous "firsts" to his credit: the first topless swimsuit, knitted tube dress, see-through clothes, unstructured bathing suit, designer jeans, and thong bathing suit. He was also the first to incorporate cutouts and make garments from plastic and vinyl. Gernreich must have had fun designing the costumes for *Skidoo*, and his style matched the film's generally outrageous tone. Carol Channing's boldly colored, feathered, sequined, and mini-skirted costumes are particularly amusing.

film poster

The poster for *Skidoo* reflects the liberated, swinging '60s. Like many of Otto Preminger's film posters, it does not use pictures of actors to sell the movie, even though the cast was a highly familiar group of stars. Preminger was one of the first directors to develop an identity for his films through his work with legendary designer Saul Bass, and took a great interest in all aspects of his films' advertising. His posters were not marketing vehicles for film stars, but rather, graphic interpretations of the story. The only indication of the movie's stars is the small pudgy cartoon character in a striped prison uniform, suggestive of Jackie Gleason. The flower-power elements are all very '60s, and though graphically interesting, tease us into believing that the film is fun, provocative, and hip. It is, unfortunately, none of those things.

TOMI UNGERER

The small character is the creation of the acclaimed artist Tomi Ungerer, who brought a whimsical element to the project. Commissioned by Preminger to create the artwork, Ungerer worked with the director and Preminger's associate, Nat Rudnick. Born in 1931 in Strasbourg, France, on the German border, Ungerer lost his father at an early age, and survived the country's occupation by German troops during WWII. In post-war France, he had little success in school and emigrated to America when he was twenty-five. Ungerer made his mark in the graphic world with his joyous, comical, endearing, sexual, absurd, and politically savvy art. He has illustrated numerous children's books, including *One Two, Where's My Shoe* (1964), *Flat Stanley* (1964), *Crictor* (1983), *Moon Man* (1984), and *Flix* (1998). The prolific artist's work has been used to advertise the *New York Times*, horseracing, cleansing products, and theater productions, among many other campaigns. His cartoons have appeared in *The New Yorker*, *Esquire*, *Life*, *Fortune*, and *Harper's*. Ungerer's anti-war political posters are among his most recognized.

Tomi Ungerer and the National Parks

In 1966, two years before *Skidoo* was released, Ungerer (as well as a number of other contemporary photographers and artists, such as Ansel Adams, Leonard Baskin, and Ben Shahn) was commissioned by the National Park Service to create posters for the country's national parks. It was the most ambitious marketing effort undertaken by the government to promote the national park system since the 1930s and the WPA. Unfortunately, the effort was suffocated by bureaucratic inertia, and Ungerer's delightful posters were never published.

THE ENFORCER

Directed by
JAMES FARGO

MALPASO/WARNER BROTHERS
96 minutes, Color

CAST

Clint Eastwood	Inspector Harry Callahan
Tyne Daly	Inspector Kate Moore
Harry Guardino	Lieutenant Al Bressler
Bradford Dillman	Captain McKay
John Mitchum	Inspector Frank DiGiorgio
Albert Popwell	Big Ed Mustapha
De Veren Bookwalter	Bobby Maxwell
John Crawford	The Mayor
Samantha Doane	Wanda
Robert F. Hoy	Buchinski
Jocelyn Jones	Miki
M.G. Kelly	Father John
Nick Pellegrino	Martin
Rudy Ramos	Mendez
Bill Ackridge	Andy
Jan Stratton	Mrs. Grey
Tim Burrus	Henry Lee
Michael Cavanaugh	Lalo
Adele Proom	Irene DiGiorgio
Brian Fong	Scoutmaster
Gloria Prince	Massage Girl
Fritz Manes	Detective #1

CREATIVE

Producer	Robert Daley
Character, Dirty Harry	Harry Julian Fink, Rita M. Fink
Screenplay	Gail Morgan Hickman, S.W. Schurr
	Stirling Silliphant, Dean Riesner
Cinematography	Charles W. Short
Editing	Joel Cox, Ferris Webster
Score	Jerry Fielding
Art Direction	Allen E. Smith
Set Decoration	Ira Bates
Costumes	Glenn Wright

CLINT EASTWOOD IS DIRTY HARRY
THE ENFORCER

CLINT EASTWOOD "THE ENFORCER" A MALPASO COMPANY FILM · Also Starring HARRY GUARDINO · BRADFORD DILLMAN · TYNE DALY · Story by GAIL MORGAN HICKMAN & S.W. SCHURR
Screenplay by STIRLING SILLIPHANT and DEAN RIESNER · Based on characters created by HARRY JULIAN FINK & R.M. FINK · Directed by JAMES FARGO · Produced by ROBERT DALEY
Music by JERRY FIELDING · PANAVISION® · Color by DELUXE® · Distributed by WARNER BROS. ⓦ A WARNER COMMUNICATIONS COMPANY

R — **RESTRICTED** — Under 17 requires accompanying Parent or Adult Guardian

THE STORY

When renegade Police Inspector Harry Callahan's over-the-top methods go too far, Police Captain McKay sends him to a desk job in the personnel department. His partner Frank is back on the street and finds a guard killed at the entrance to an ammunitions warehouse. Frank and his new partner sneak up on the gang, but in the shoot-out that ensues, Frank is mortally wounded and his partner is killed. The gang drives off with the munitions, including the new Laws supersonic rocket.

The gun thieves (calling themselves the People's Revolutionary Strike Force) kidnap the mayor and threaten to bomb San Francisco if they don't get $5 million. Harry is put on the case and assigned a new partner, rookie Inspector Kate Moore, whom Harry snubs because she is a woman. Harry and Kate are attending the autopsy of Frank's partner when a bomb goes off. Harry recognizes a man running from the scene and chases him through San Francisco, finally catching him inside a church, where a young priest, Father John, tries to protect him. They find out the bomber's name is Henry Lee Caldwell, thought to be a black militant associated with a group run by Big Ed Mustapha.

Harry and Kate go to Mustapha, who tells them about Henry Lee's militant Vietnam vet buddy, Bobby Maxwell, and a woman named Wanda, who works at Tiffany's brothel. Harry visits the brothel and finds out that Wanda had left two weeks earlier because she found religion at the same church where Harry found Henry Lee. Harry goes to the church and confronts Father John. The priest knows Henry Lee and Bobby Maxwell from San Quentin, where he worked in prisoner rehabilitation. Unbeknownst to Harry, Wanda is aiming a gun at him. A shot is fired, but it's from Kate's gun, and she's killed Wanda. A distraught Father John confesses that the gang took the mayor and the guns to Alcatraz.

Harry and Kate take a fireboat to Alcatraz. Kate goes up to the cellhouse as Harry hunts down the gang. As Kate rounds A Block, she sees one of the gang, Lalo, holding the mayor. She tells Lalo to release the mayor and when he laughs at her, she kills him on the spot. As she rushes the mayor out of the cellhouse, Kate sees Harry, but suddenly she spots Bobby Maxwell aiming a gun at them. She yells to Harry, who backs away, then pushes the mayor aside—and in that moment, she is in the open, a perfect target for the gunman. Bobby shoots her, then grabs the mayor and heads off to the guard tower. Harry goes to Kate and she dies in his arms.

Bobby desperately climbs the guard tower and leaves the mayor mid-way as he runs to the top. Bobby yells for his gang, but Harry and Kate have killed them all. Harry picks up the Laws rocket Bobby dropped, takes direct aim, and fires. The huge rocket spirals toward Bobby, exploding on impact and blowing off the entire top of the tower. Helicopters circle the island as Harry stands on the steps of the prison buildling above Kate's dead body.

PRISON ADMINISTRATION BUILDING—*INSPECTOR KATE MOORE (TYNE DALY) IS SHOT AND DIES HERE.*

THE INSIDE SCOOP

Third in the *"Dirty Harry"* series, *The Enforcer* is true to the brand: it's fast, explosive, and funny. Within the series, *The Enforcer* is the most easy-going and sexually provocative. The character of *Dirty Harry* was the creation of husband-and-wife team Harry and Rita Fink, with screenwriter Dean Riesner. Harry Callahan is a prototypical action hero—an iconoclastic loner, as contemptuous of government bureaucracy and corruption as he is unflinching and resolute in his battles with criminals. We root for Harry Callahan, regardless of his tactics, because he's incorruptible. When Mustapha asks Harry why he is so determined, he replies, "You wouldn't believe me if I told you," implying that he's motivated not by fame or fortune, but by a desire for justice, even if (or particularly if) it's his idea of justice. Eastwood is known for having significant say in his movies, and *The Enforcer* is a Clint Eastwood film, produced by his company, Malpaso, with a director hand-picked and a script approved by Eastwood.

In *The Enforcer*, Eastwood presents the character we've come to expect, one whose outrageous actions, though predictable, are still exciting. However, it's his relationship with the spunky Kate Moore character that is most intriguing, and distinguishes *The Enforcer* from the other films in the series. Caught off-guard by her overt flirting and her courage, Callahan's uncharacteristic reactions reveal a softer side to Dirty Harry that we've not seen before. Their pairing, though doomed, is a touching and welcome surprise. Her character showed, for the first time, that a woman could be as tough, capable, and determined a police officer as a man, especially über-cop Harry Callahan. Kate demonstrates that cops are as complex and vulnerable as everyone else. Despite the fact that Moore wears a skirt while chasing criminals around the city, she is steadfast and dependable. She saves Harry's life not once, but twice, and "takes the bullet" in the end. She is the film's true hero.

Two important stories from the '70s play into *The Enforcer*: the Symbionese Liberation Army (SLA), and the Vietnam War. In April 1974 (two years before the film was released), Patty Hearst and a group identifying themselves as members of the SLA were caught on videotape robbing a bank in San Francisco. The group's "mission" was to start a revolution of the underprivileged by declaring war on those with status and money. A year later, in April 1975, America's involvement in Vietnam ended and the horror stories and nightmares suffered by our soldiers became increasingly more public. *The Enforcer* combines the displaced, traumatized Vietnam veteran and the radical revolutionary into the militarily trained People's Revolutionary Strike Force. This story line is not the film's strongest element, and the hippie-headband Strike Force is a ragtag group of comic proportions. However, it does offer Harry a psychotic enemy with firearms experience. (A similar and far more powerful Alcatraz–military connection would reappear two decades later in *The Rock*.)

the studio: WARNER BROTHERS

In the early '50s, as television became a ubiquitous fixture in American homes, there was a downturn in the movie business. Older brothers Harry and Albert Warner retired, and by the end of the decade, Warner Brothers began losing money for the first time in twenty years. Then, younger brother Jack was bought out by Seven Arts in 1967, and Warner–Seven Arts was born; two years later, the giant Kinney National Services Corporation took over. Warner Brothers, now part of Warner Communications, was headed by Ted Ashley, with John Calley in charge of production, and Clint Eastwood's friend and former lawyer, Frank Wells, overseeing the business end. The new team rescued the studio. The *"Dirty Harry"* series was part of Warner's success in the '70s and '80s, and *The Enforcer* did more business than its predecessors, *Dirty Harry* (1971) and *Magnum Force* (1973), earning $46 million at the box-office. Made at a cost of $4 million, *The Enforcer* became Warner's seventeenth biggest moneymaker of the decade.

MALPASO PRODUCTIONS

The Enforcer was produced by Eastwood's Malpaso Production Company (its fourteenth film) and Warner Brothers, who produced and distributed the original *Dirty Harry* in 1971 as well as all four sequels. In the late '60s, as Eastwood's fame and box-office draw began to skyrocket, he formed his own production company, which he named Malpaso Productions after a small river on his property in Monterey County. Malpaso allowed Eastwood to have complete oversight of his movies, with control over scripts, directors, and casting. As the principal shareholder, Eastwood also reaped the financial benefits of his on-screen success.

"What we got here is a well organized group of militants with enough explosives to blow up San Francisco."

Captain McKay, *The Enforcer*

DOCK, LOOKING TOWARD BAY BRIDGE

DIRTY HARRY

By the time *The Enforcer* hit the screen in 1976, five years and two sequels after *Dirty Harry*, "Harry Callahan" and Clint Eastwood had achieved international fame. Eastwood is in top form in *The Enforcer*, aided by a caustic and funny script by Sterling Silliphant and Dean Riesner, but he was not the first choice to play the unconventional policeman. *Dirty Harry* (1971) was first offered to Paul Newman, who had philosophical problems with a character who disdained police and legal procedures and used violence to counteract violence. Frank Wells then brought it to Eastwood, but he was committed to finishing his first directorial effort, *Play Misty for Me* (1971). Frank Sinatra was offered the role, but an injury made him unavailable. It eventually got back to Eastwood, who by that time had finished *Misty*. Eastwood brought in Don Siegel and in turn, Dean Riesner. San Francisco was also not first on the list of possible film locales. The original story was set in New York City, and then Seattle was briefly considered. San Francisco was chosen in large part because the filmmakers wanted to use the soon-to-be-torn-down Kezar Stadium for the first *Dirty Harry's* final showdown.

Eastwood and *Dirty Harry* received tremendous criticism in the '70s when these films were released, in large part because his outrageous and violent tactics completely disregarded the rights of an alleged criminal. His aim was to rid society of evil by any means possible, to hell with the law and the Constitution. The social revolution that began in the '60s was changing our nation, and the conflict in Vietnam galvanized many young people to speak out against what they considered to be the government's misguided military activities. As the country entered the '70s, it was a more socially aware nation; in this context, *Dirty Harry* was not a hero to be admired. Today, these films are generally viewed less critically, seen as good action pictures rather than serious social statements.

ALCATRAZ: REEL TO REAL

The infamous decaying federal penitentiary on Alcatraz was an ideal location for the film's climactic final sequence. When Eastwood and Daly board a boat and head to the island for the final showdown, the prison looms larger and larger in their view; Daly says, "Alcatraz," and with that single word, evokes the power of the prison's notorious past. By the time *The Enforcer* was released in 1976, the island had been part of the Golden Gate National Recreation Area for three years, and was open to visitors, who lined up to see the Rock first-hand, and take ranger-led tours. At that time, it was possible for filmmakers to buy out tickets to the island, which allowed *The Enforcer*'s cast and crew unencumbered access. (This practice had been discontinued by the time Eastwood made *Escape from Alcatraz* three years later, and for that movie, the filmmakers were forced to work with and around park visitors.) The popularity of *The Enforcer* gave millions of movie-goers one of their first inside views of the infamous prison.

The final scene in which Harry blows off the top of the guard tower is well remembered by visitors, some of whom ask to see the guard tower that was blown-up. The faux guard tower constructed by Paramount Pictures was made from balsa wood, Styrofoam, and metal, and sited where no tower had ever actually existed, near the residential end of the island, on the grounds of the bluff by Windy Gulch below the lighthouse. The fake guard tower was so authentic-looking that a high-ranking NPS official initially accused the park of allowing the movie company to destroy an historic structure. Visitors can see one of the prison's original towers, standing on the island's eastern side near the dock as it has since the 1940s.

PRISON CELLS

STARRING

CLINT EASTWOOD (Harry Callahan) was already a star in 1971 when he took on the namesake role in the first of the *"Dirty Harry"* series, but after the film's release in December of that year, Eastwood became—and remains—an international superstar. His trademark sneer, caustic remarks, and deadpan delivery have become the stuff of movie legend.

Eastwood is a native of San Francisco, born in 1930 when Alcatraz was still a military prison and four years before it became a federal penitentiary. His father was a steel worker and the family moved around often looking for work. Jazz was an early and important influence on Eastwood. He tried to enroll at Seattle University, which had a noted music program, but he was drafted instead, and was sent to Fort Ord in California. After his two years of service were complete, he went to L.A. City College and enrolled in business administration, but never finished. He had met actors while in the military, including Martin Milner and David Janssen, and was introduced to what would become his life work. He got a contract with Universal for $75 a week and was given acting lessons. Eastwood's first role was as a lab technician in the sci-fi feature *Revenge of the Creature* (1955, a sequel to the far superior *Creature from the Black Lagoon*, 1954). Four years later, after parts in less than a dozen movies, he turned to television, where he played Rowdy Yates in the popular Western television series *Rawhide*. In 1964, Eastwood went to Europe to star as the stoic and vengeful "man with no name" in Italian director Sergio Leone's first "spaghetti" western, *A Fistful of Dollars*. It was a risky move for the television actor, but the role allowed him to reinvent his Hollywood image. Eastwood's cool, laconic performance and striking screen presence dominated the film. Eastwood also starred in Leone's sequels, *For a Few Dollars More* (1965), and his masterpiece, *The Good, the Bad, and the Ugly* (1966). Leone's re-imagining of the Western film genre and an exceptional score by Ennio Morricone were huge hits, and Clint Eastwood became a genuine movie star.

In the ten years between 1971 and 1980, Eastwood had three of Warner Brothers' top twenty money-makers: *The Enforcer* (1976), $46 million; *Every Which Way But Loose* (1978), $51 million; and *Any Which Way You Can* (1980), $39.5 million. Three years after *The Enforcer*, Eastwood would score a huge success in the quintessential Alcatraz film, *Escape from Alcatraz*, forever solidifying his connection to the Rock.

TYNE DALY's (Kate Moore) role in *The Enforcer* was her breakthrough part. It was Daly's first starring screen performance—and only fifth motion picture—and she received second billing at Eastwood's insistence. Daly turned down the role of Kate Moore three times before being convinced that the character would not be used as comic relief. It was the first time a woman was portrayed as a worthy partner to Harry Callahan (or any previous film detective, for that matter). Daly was Eastwood's choice, selected over other more traditionally glamorous actresses. Daly is great, especially at showing sensitivity in violent and frightening situations. Eastwood doesn't flinch in the face of fear, but Daly realistically and compassionately shows what seem to be the real emotions that come with the job.

Daly's role as Police Inspector Kate Moore was not an anomaly for her. Among her many successes were seven years as police inspector Mary Beth Lacey on TV's first female-cop buddy series *Cagney and Lacey*. Her other television credits include *Christy* (1994–1995) and *Judging Amy* (1999–2005). Daly has received 10 Emmy nominations and four awards. Film, television, and musical theater actress Tyne Daly is among the most versatile of her generation.

ALBERT POPWELL (Big Ed Mustapha) is an elegant actor, giving a smooth, confident portrayal as the head of a black militant group. He is the only character that Callahan respects (aside from his partner Kate). Popwell starred in the first four *Dirty Harry* pictures, portraying a bank robber (*Dirty Harry*, 1971), a pimp (*Magnum Force*, 1973), and a black militant (*The Enforcer*, 1976), before turning to law enforcement, playing Harry's partner in *Sudden Impact* (1983). Popwell was known for his role as Matthew Johnson in the '70s *Cleopatra Jones* films.

BRADFORD DILLMAN (Captain McKay) is convincingly slimy in *The Enforcer*, playing an over-the-top bureaucrat more interested in his career than in his duty, the type of man Harry Callahan despises. Dillman started his career auspiciously at 28, when he worked at 20th Century Fox for celebrated directors Jean Negulesco, Tony Richardson, and Michael Curtiz. At Fox, he made his mark playing criminal Artie Straus in the film *Compulsion* (1959), based on the infamous Leopold and Loeb murder trial, which focused on two wealthy and brilliant law students who believed they could get away with murder.

HARRY GUARDINO (Lieutenant Al Bressler) reprises his role as the understanding, but tough Lt. Bressler in *The Enforcer*, after having played him in Don Siegel's original *Dirty Harry* (1971). He received great reviews for his roles in the family comedy *Houseboat* (1958) with Cary Grant and Sophia Loren. His tough guy roles include Lewis Milestone's *Pork Chop Hill* (1959); Martin Ritt's *5 Branded Women* (1960); and two Don Siegel hits, *Hell is for Heroes* (1962) and *Madigan* (1968). In 1975 Guardino starred with Ben Gazarra in the film *Capone*.

Big Ed Mustapha:
"You really are a dirty bastard, ain't you Harry?"

Lt. Harry Callahan:
"The dirtiest"

BEHIND THE SCENES

Director JAMES FARGO was given his first directorial responsibility on *The Enforcer*, after working as assistant director on four Eastwood films, *Joe Kidd* (1972), *High Plains Drifter* (1973), *The Eiger Sanction* (1975), and *The Outlaw Josey Wales* (1976). Fargo keeps the tone of the *Dirty Harry* franchise, but his direction lacks the hard edge that Siegel brought to the earlier pictures. The opening sequence—which features Harry driving his car through a storefront—is wonderfully entertaining, as is the final shoot-out on Alcatraz. The plot of *The Enforcer* is not particularly strong, but Fargo provides good action and chase sequences, keeping the banter fun, and giving generous time to the tender scenes between Eastwood and Daly. Fargo directed a number of action films and TV shows, and again directed Eastwood in one of his most commercially successful films, *Every Which Way But Loose* (1978).

Writers HARRY JULIAN FINK and **RITA M. FINK** created the *Dirty Harry* character and the story and screenplay for the original 1971 film. Together, they also wrote the John Wayne film *Big Jake* (1971). Harry wrote the screen story for *Ice Station Zebra* (1968) and earlier, for television shows *Kraft Television Theater* (1947), *The Rifleman* (1958), and *Ben Casey* (1961).

Screenwriters GAIL MORGAN HICKMAN and **S. W. SCHURR** wrote the original script for *The Enforcer* (then called *Moving Target*) when they were film students in San Francisco. They managed to get the script (their first) to Eastwood through his restaurant, Hog's Breath, in Carmel. Hickman also wrote the screenplays for the Charles Bronson films, *Murphy's Law* (1986) and *Death Wish 4: The Crackdown* (1987).

Screenwriters DEAN RIESNER and **STERLING SILLIPHANT'S** dialogue for *The Enforcer* keeps the movie snappy even when the story line lacks credibility. Riesner worked on the original *Dirty Harry* screenplay, as well as two other Clint Eastwood films, *Play Misty for Me* (1971), and *High Plains Drifter* (1973). He became known as a script doctor, hired to polish other writers' movies. Silliphant was responsible for suggesting Eastwood have a female partner in *The Enforcer*, which became crucial to the film. He was a prolific writer, turning out a plethora of screenplays, television shows, and novels over the course of his career. His television work included four years and over seventy episodes of *Route 66* (1960–1964). He won an Oscar for *In the Heat of the Night* (1967). His other films include *The Lineup*, directed by Don Siegel (1958), *Charly* (1968), and *The Towering Inferno* (1974). Both men worked as writers on the television series *Rawhide* (1959–66), in which Eastwood starred.

INSIDE CELLHOUSE, C BLOCK

Editors JOEL COX and **FERRIS WEBSTER** worked together on five Eastwood films, starting with *The Enforcer* (1976), through *The Gauntlet* (1977), *Every Which Way But Loose* (1978), *Bronco Billy* (1980), and *Honkytonk Man* (1982)—Webster's last film. Webster was one of the great Hollywood film editors (see the *Escape from Alcatraz* entry for more information), and mentored Cox as they collaborated on Eastwood's films. Cox is now Eastwood's primary film editor, having worked on eighteen films and winning an Oscar for Eastwood's celebrated Western, *Unforgiven* (1992).

Composer JERRY FIELDING created an elegant, urban jazz score for *The Enforcer*. Fielding's music beautifully enhances the film and is particularly effective in the chase sequences through San Francisco. Fielding received three Oscar nominations, two for Sam Peckinpah's *The Wild Bunch* (1970) and *Straw Dogs* (1971), and one for Eastwood's *The Outlaw Josey Wales* (1976). Fielding worked throughout his career on top television shows including *Star Trek*, *Shane*, and *Mission Impossible* (all 1966). In 1979, Fielding scored another Eastwood-and-Alcatraz film, *Escape from Alcatraz*.

film poster

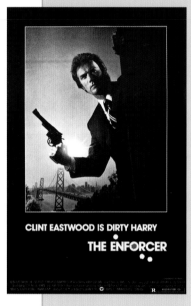

CLINT EASTWOOD IS DIRTY HARRY
•
THE ENFORCER
• •

Designer BILL GOLD was behind the dynamic posters for many of Eastwood's films, beginning with his directorial debut, *Play Misty for Me* (1971), and including the famous *"Dirty Harry"* series. Like Preminger and Hitchcock before him, both of whom worked with designer Saul Bass, Eastwood takes a direct interest in all aspects of his films, an interest that extends to the way they are advertised and promoted. As a result, he has developed long-term relationships with specific designers. Gold was one of many talented artists in Hollywood during the '30s, participating in the crafting of huge advertising campaigns for films. Gold's illustrious Hollywood career spanned five decades—he was behind the classic poster for *Casablanca* (1942), among many others. Working with Eastwood, Gold helped define the actor/director's movie image. The posters in the *"Dirty Harry"* series are surprisingly elegant and contemporary in their spare and streamlined design, and all feature Clint Eastwood and his infamous (and enormous) .44 Magnum, reinforcing Dirty Harry as one of the most familiar characters in movie history.

The posters for the first three *"Dirty Harry"* films, *Dirty Harry* (1971), *Magnum Force* (1973), and *The Enforcer* (1976), display a similar striking design quality. Gold chose black-and-white photographs, when most movie posters made in the '70s were dominated by colorful art. The original *Dirty Harry* poster uses yellow and pink shading over Eastwood shooting his .44 Magnum, with text that reads: *"Detective Harry Callahan. He doesn't break murder cases. He smashes them."* With the second *"Dirty Harry"* film, *Magnum Force*, released two years later, Gold dispensed with lead-in copy and the only color was in the title *Magnum Force*, which was printed in red. A year later, when *The Enforcer* was released, the poster style was simplified even further. Gold dispensed with color entirely except for a red drop of blood replacing the "o" in Enforcer, creating a beautiful and imposing image. The only copy reads: *"Clint Eastwood is Dirty Harry."* That says it all.

GUARD TOWER, EASTERN SIDE OF ISLAND

ESCAPE FROM ALCATRAZ

Directed by
DON SIEGEL

MALPASO/PARAMOUNT
112 minutes, Color

CAST

Clint Eastwood	Frank Morris
Patrick McGoohan	Warden
Paul Benjamin	English
Robert Blossom	Doc
Jack Thibeau	Clarence Anglin
Fred Ward	John Anglin
Larry Hankin	Charley Butts
Bruce M. Fischer	Wolf
Frank Ronzio	Litmus
Regina Baff	Lucy (Mrs. Charley Butts)
Candace Bowen	English's Daughter
Danny Glover	Inmate (film debut)

CREATIVE

Executive Producer	Robert Daley
Associate Producer	Fritz Manes
Producer	Don Siegel
Novel	J. Campbell Bruce
Screenplay	Richard Tuggle
Cinematography	Bruce Surtees
Editing	Ferris Webster
Composer	Jerry Fielding
Set Decoration	Edward J. McDonald

"No one has ever escaped from Alcatraz...and no one ever will."

CLINT EASTWOOD
ESCAPE FROM
ALCATRAZ

OPENS FRIDAY, JUNE 22nd AT A THEATRE NEAR YOU.

Convict Frank Morris is transported by barge to America's toughest prison, USP Alcatraz, where he goes through the rough induction process, guarded every step of the way until he is locked in a cell. The next morning, he joins the other convicts, beginning their daily routine by walking single file to the dining hall.

Morris's first work assignment is in the prison library. Time passes, and as he delivers books to prisoners, he begins to understand the routines and monotony of life on the Rock. After watching a cockroach climb through a grate into the back wall of his cell, he tests the concrete and finds that it crumbles easily.

In the mess hall, Morris and his neighbor Charlie Butts sit with two new prisoners, brothers Clarence and John Anglin. Morris tells them he's figured out a way to escape. First, they'll dig out the air vents in the back of their cells and climb into the space behind, which leads to the top of the cell house. At the top is a vent that opens to the roof, from the roof they can go down to the ground, and then head to the water.

Morris tells the group about a flotation device made out of raincoats he read about. If they leave at night, patrols are few, but they'll need to create fake heads to place on their pillows. The men agree to the plan. To camouflage their work, they need something to block the wall; Morris orders an accordion.

Over time, the four men dig out their grates, build fake covers to hide their work, and create dummy heads out of scraps of paper, water, and barbershop sweepings. When Morris finishes his head and can squeeze through the grate, he tests his plan. All goes well until he reaches the ceiling, where he finds that the ventilator hole is sealed. During music rehearsals, Morris steals a fan and from it, devises a drill to loosen the ceiling cover. The plan is set and all four men are ready to go.

It's Monday morning and the men are in the mess hall. The escape is set for Tuesday night. The warden, also in the mess hall, sees another prisoner, Litmus, sitting with the group, holding a chrysanthemum. He walks to their table, grabs the flower, and crushes it. Litmus is shocked. He becomes overwhelmed, grabs his chest, and suffers a fatal heart attack. "Some men are destined never to leave Alcatraz alive," the warden sneers, staring at Morris. Suspicious of Morris, the warden instructs a guard to change his cell in the morning, which would foil their plans. Luckily, Morris is anxious as well, and they decide not to wait, but to escape that night.

When the lights go out, Frank and the Anglin brothers are ready to go, but Butts panics and can't leave. The three men slip through their vents into the utility corridor, and upwards to the roof. Climbing down to the ground, they run silently to the island's north shore, blow air into their makeshift rafts, and float away. The next morning, guards discover the fake heads, and a massive search ensues. Law enforcement agencies were certain they would find the bodies. They never did.

INSIDE CELLHOUSE, "BROADWAY," *YELLLOW LINES PAINTED ON BY FILMMAKERS*

THE INSIDE SCOOP

Escape from Alcatraz is a quintessential prison film and the best Hollywood movie ever made about the federal penitentiary on Alcatraz Island. Not only is it a thrilling story, it's based on the island's most famous escape attempt. Director Don Siegel handles the material expertly, starting with a stunning opening sequence where Eastwood is taken brusquely through his induction into prison, through to the climactic escape from Alcatraz.

When Paramount Pictures was offered *Escape from Alcatraz* directed by Don Siegel, they gave it a green light even before seeing a script. Siegel brought in Eastwood, and movie history was ready to be made. What could be more dynamic or marketable then Eastwood's commanding screen presence, Siegel's sharp direction, and the notorious Alcatraz Island. In true Hollywood fashion, this ideal pairing almost didn't happen. Before filming began, Siegel and Eastwood had a falling out. Both men had considerable power in Hollywood and, it was said, neither was willing to give up control of the film. Siegel even went so far as to approach other actors about the role, but none signed on. With time running out, Siegel went to Eastwood, the men reconciled, and a deal was struck. Siegel and Eastwood knew each other well, having worked together on four previous films, including the original *Dirty Harry* (1971). *Escape* would be their last collaboration.

The director was not new to the prison genre. Twenty-five years earlier, Siegel had made the acclaimed prison film, *Riot in Cellblock 11* (1954), highlighting harsh conditions inside an American prison. In *Escape*, Siegel presents a clinical look at the daily lives of Alcatraz prisoners, revealing the island's inner life, and the systems that keep it going. Scenes of head counts, single-file marches, and walks through metal detectors unveil the tedium of time on the Rock. A prisoner describes the monotony of these routines: "We count the hours, the bulls count us, and the king bulls count the counts." Siegel uses this consistency to create obstacles for Morris to overcome, building tension with each successive day as the prisoners figure out how to undermine the system.

In comparison to other big star-powered films of 1979, including, *Alien*, *Apocalypse Now*, and *Moonraker*, *Escape from Alcatraz* was unusually austere. A slow-moving prison drama without much action, realistically filmed in dull, fog-inspired colors with a subtle undertone of music and minimal dialogue, *Escape* would appear to have been without box-office appeal. But Siegel created a compelling film by establishing Alcatraz as an imposing fortress, its warden as a ruthless disciplinarian, and the prison as a series of routines calibrated to conquer the prisoners' spirits. The film wastes no time in getting to the escape plan and, once set in motion, Eastwood's magnetic screen presence carries us step-by-step to the finish. It's a simple and striking achievement

"The way I figure it, the cell block is really getting old, and the moist air is corroding the concrete, and salt is rusting the metal."

Frank Morris, *Escape from Alcatraz*

For all its austerity, *Escape* is still a Hollywood movie, presenting the inmates as decent, likeable men, and building sympathetic relationships between them. We are encouraged to root for these convicts against a brutal prison system, especially one run by a callous warden, diabolically overplayed by Patrick McGoohan. In fact, except for one sexual aggressor, Wolf, none of the prisoners appear at all threatening. Old-timer Doc is a sensitive painter. Sweet, plump Litmus brings comic relief with his penchant for desserts and his pet mouse. Fatherly English, a "lifer", brings wisdom to their isolated world. Eastwood's Morris is the most dangerous character, because his mind is more active and creative then those of the island's other prisoners or guards. He uses this power to look out for fellow inmates, bridge the racial divide with English, stand up to the warden, and finally, escape from Alcatraz. Eastwood is the hero.

Filming on Alcatraz was arduous: the weather was chilling, the fog was damp, and the raucous gulls were everywhere. Exacerbating these conditions, fans eager to see movie stars often interrupted shooting. By mid-October 1973, Alcatraz Island was part of the national park system, and National Park Service rangers welcomed visitors to the infamous prison. Eastwood was able to quell these crowds with the promise of autographs, but eventually filming was switched to non-visiting hours. Regardless of the hardships, shooting on the island and inside the prison made *Escape from Alcatraz* a benchmark in the Alcatraz-and-Hollywood story; it was the first film to reveal the inner workings of the once-mysterious Rock to audiences all over the world. *Escape from Alcatraz* was the fifteenth top-grossing film of 1979, earning $43 million at the box office. The film's title has become part of the American vernacular and its enduring success continues to promote international interest in the island, which is today one of the major tourist destinations in the United States.

the studio: PARAMOUNT PICTURES AND MALPASO PRODUCTIONS

When Don Siegel bought the film rights to *Escape from Alcatraz*, the studio most appropriate to steward the project was Warner Brothers, where the two men had worked on the *Dirty Harry* series, but following a falling out between Siegel and Eastwood over control of the film, Siegel took the property to Paramount. In the early 1970s, Paramount Pictures had once again become Hollywood's biggest movie studio. *Escape from Alcatraz* was produced by Clint Eastwood's **Malpaso Productions**. Executive producer Robert Daley and associate producer Fritz Manes, who worked exclusively for Malpaso, were behind many of Eastwood's films in the 1970s and '80s.

ALCATRAZ: REEL TO REAL

In the opening scene, the boat bringing Morris to Alcatraz is named the *Warden Johnston* after the first warden of Alcatraz, James A. Johnston (warden, 1934–1948). The filmmakers were able to acquire the actual boat authorities used to transport prisoners, island staff, and families during all the federal penitentiary years.

The film was made on Alcatraz Island during the summer of 1978. The film company repainted "Broadway," the dining room, and D Block for use in the movie, as well as painting yellow lines (which did not exist historically) along Broadway and chiseling holes in the back walls of four C-Block cells, #111, #113, #119, #121. The cells used for the filming of *Escape from Alcatraz* were different than those of the real Morris and Anglin brothers. Morris and the Anglins were housed on the bottom row of B Block, in cells #138, #140, and #144. In the film, they used cells located in the C Block, the middle cells on the "Broadway" side, along the bottom row.

Portions of the cell sequences in *Escape from Alcatraz* were filmed on a studio back-lot using an authentic recreation of the prison. These sets were especially crucial for shots in the small cell when Eastwood was shown digging, and when the men are climbing inside the utility corridor.

The studio recreated some of the cell furnishings, which they left behind. Metal plates in the kitchen, a portable metal detector at the entrance to the mess hall, and many of the prison's cell cots were among the items that remained on the island. The cots were not replicas of Alcatraz prison cots, but were instead WWII-vintage cots from an army barracks and quite different from the style used in the prison.

In the movie, Doc, a prisoner who paints, chops his fingers off while at work in the Model Industries building when his painting privilege is revoked. This is loosely based on Rufe Persful (#284), who in the 1930s, chopped off four of his fingers with a fire ax. Persful, a "convict-guard" at notorious Tucker State Farm in Arkansas, shot a fellow prisoner trying to escape a chain gang. His reputation followed him to Alcatraz, where he rationally came to the conclusion that the only way to survive the death threats he received from other prisoners was to commit an irrational act and maim himself. He was transferred to the safety of a prison hospital at Springfield, MO, and was eventually released. He died at an old age.

There was an attempt to duplicate the 1962 escape at Lompoc Federal Prison after the film *Escape from Alcatraz* was shown there. The inmate even constructed a dummy head, but was caught before he had a chance to attempt the escape. (Most films shown to prison populations were of a more tame variety.)

THE MORRIS–ANGLIN ESCAPE

DUMMY HEADS USED IN ESCAPE, ESCAPE ROUTE

DUMMY HEAD ON BED, CELL WITH DUMMY HEAD ON BED, FAKE AIR VENT COVER ON BED

CORRECTIONAL OFFICERS: IN ESCAPE CELL, IN UTILITY CORRIDOR BEHIND ESCAPE CELL,
ON ROOF WHERE ESCAPEES CLIMBED OUT

THE REAL FRANK MORRIS

Frank Lee Morris (Alcatraz #1441) was a career burglar and escape artist; convicted of his first crime at age thirteen, Morris escaped (and was caught) several times from the National Training School for Boys, an industrial school for juvenile "delinquents"; several times from Florida State Prison at Raiford; and from Louisiana State Prison, Angola, to which he was never returned. In his last offense, on September 19, 1956, Morris and accomplices bored a hole in the back of a Louisiana bank, burned into two vaults, and stole twenty-six sacks of coins worth $6,165. Caught, convicted, and sent to USP Atlanta, Morris was captured trying to escape from that institution, and that—coupled with his previous escape record— earned him a transfer to Alcatraz. Records indicate that Morris had no family and that throughout his childhood he was shuffled among foster homes. Morris was thought to have a superior IQ (134-136).

THE MORRIS–ANGLIN ESCAPE

In the actual 1962 attempt, Morris and his conspirators took seven months to design and execute their plan. Morris, who had escaped from other prisons, was the purported architect behind the plan, though Allen Clayton West (the

CLARENCE ANGLIN, JOHN ANGLIN, FRANK MORRIS

model for the "Charlie Butts" character), the only member who did not escape, later told the FBI that he was the mastermind. According to Alcatraz historian Jolene Babyak, it was likely that both Morris and West were in charge by virtue of their intelligence and cunning. As Babyak puts it, "Since West was one of the cellhouse maintenance men (he painted the ceilings and got on top of the "block" to the exit vents) he had the widest circulation, and could pick up tools, cement powder (for the masks), paint (for the cell walls and fake walls), electrical wires (for the interior of the masks and later used to drop the raft and life jackets down from the roof), blankets (to hide the work on top of the block), barber clippers, even a vacuum cleaner motor (which was never used because it was too loud, but was found with other items). His friends who aided were Carnes (cellhouse librarian), Bumpy Johnston (cellhouse maintenance), and Glenn May (cellhouse electrician who provided wire and may have made two of the masks). This was a cellhouse escape plan and West had the run of the cellhouse". Though West did not escape, he did provide authorities with specific information about its planning and execution, including the use of soap and toilet paper to create the dummy heads, and camouflage for the vents they dug out. He also said they used glue stolen from the glove shop to bond the raincoats for flotation devices. As in the movie, the prisoners were never found, though authorities believe they did not survive. Rising costs and a deteriorating prison forced USP Alcatraz to close less than a year later.

STARRING

CLINT EASTWOOD (Frank Morris) is ideally cast as convict Frank Morris, creating a character whose intelligence and determination never wavers. His understated performance is a perfect match to Siegel's sharp, almost documentary style. Following a long line of movie screen tough-guys—James Cagney, Edward G. Robinson, and Humphrey Bogart—who spent time behind bars, Eastwood revives the genre with an impressive and powerful performance.

From the film's riviting opening scene, which follows Eastwood as he is brusquely manhandled through the induction process, his performance (he's in almost every scene) sets the tone for the film. Eastwood's impenetrable gaze shows no fear. He understands he's in a situation he cannot control, and although he's resigned to the humiliation, he's not intimidated by it. Eastwood follows the prison's regimented daily routine, biding his time and carefully plotting his escape. He uses his intellect, as his weapon. Through many quiet moments, we watch Eastwood slowly solder an implement for digging, stubbornly chip away at the walls of his cell, and silently make his dummy head as the escape comes into focus. His approach is pragmatic and deliberate, reflecting the real Frank Morris's high IQ.

Eastwood's movie career took off after he made three "spaghetti' westerns with Sergio Leone in the 1960s, and after playing Inspector Harry Callahan in the *Dirty Harry* series directed by Don Siegel. Callahan is a renegade cop who loathes bureaucracy and takes the law into his own hands. Eastwood's role in *Escape from Alcatraz* is another renegade, though this time he's on the other side of the system, behind bars and defying the prison system by attempting to escape. Eastwood completely dominates the film with his quiet, confident portrayal of criminal mastermind Frank Morris.

Actor, director, producer, and composer, Clint Eastwood has reached the highest echelon in the movie business. His many notable films include *High Plains Drifter* (1973), *Every Which Way But Loose* (1978), *Bronco Billy* (1980), *Bird* (1988), *Bridges of Madison County* (1995), and *Space Cowboys* (2000). In 1992, Eastwood won Oscars for Best Director and Best Picture for his Western, *Unforgiven*; received acclaim in 2003 for directing the crime drama, *Mystic River*; and won Oscars for Best Picture and Director for the tough and heartbreaking boxing film, *Million Dollar Baby* (2004).

PATRICK MCGOOHAN (Warden) portrays the Alcatraz warden with over-the-top malice, establishing himself as the enemy and promoting the film's anti-prison position. McGoohan became famous for his television role in *Secret Agent* (UK, early '60s), and in the British sensation, *The Prisoner* (UK, 1967). McGoohan easily switched between theater, film, and television, winning two Emmys. His other films include *Ice Station Zebra* (1968), *Silver Streak* (1976), and *Braveheart* (1995).

PAUL BENJAMIN's (English) performance as a "lifer" con provides Eastwood's Morris with a confidant, one equal in authority and intelligence to himself. Benjamin's quietly defiant portrayal gracefully speaks to the injustice of a racially biased country. Benjamin's films include *Across 110th Street* (1972), *Leadbelly* (1976), *Do the Right Thing* (1989), and the indie hit *The Station Agent* (2003).

FRED WARD (John Anglin) made his American film debut in *Escape from Alcatraz* as one of the scrappy Anglin brothers. Ward's sixty films include *The Right Stuff* (1983), *Big Business* (1988), *Henry and June* (1990), *The Player* and *Bob Roberts* (both 1992), *Short Cuts* (1993), and *Sweet Home Alabama* (2002).

ROBERT BLOSSOM (Doc) brings a stark realism to his portrayal of Doc, the old-timer who finds his only joy in painting. Of all the characters, Blossom most painfully embodies a prisoner's life, a forgotten man, gaunt, pale, and hollow from his years on the Rock. His violent reaction when he's denied his painting privileges is one the film's most chilling moments. A well-known stage actor, Blossom came to film at age forty-seven in the movie *The Hospital* (1971), followed by *Slaughterhouse-Five* (1972), *The Great Gatsby* (1974), *Close Encounters of the Third Kind* (1977), *The Last Temptation of Christ* (1988), and *Home Alone* (1990).

BEHIND THE SCENES

Director **DON SIEGEL** was known for his action films, directing forty-four pictures over the course of five decades. In 1954, he made his first impression with the exciting prison drama *Riot in Cell Block 11*, produced by Walter Wanger. He worked again with Wanger on the classic sci-fi thriller *Invasions of the Body Snatchers* (1956). Siegel's films include *Baby Face Nelson* (1957), *Hell Is for Heroes* (1962), *The Killers* (1964), and *The Shootist* (1976). Siegel's film noir classic *The Lineup* (1958), was filmed in San Francisco and features a foot chase through Sutro Baths and a car chase on an unfinished Embarcadero Freeway.

Siegel first worked with Eastwood on *Coogan's Bluff* (1968), an urban-cowboy/cop movie that transitioned Eastwood from his spaghetti Westerns to a laconic hero and sex symbol. However, it was the 1971 smash *Dirty Harry* (1971) that cemented both men's reputations. Their next film together was *Escape from Alcatraz*, a perfect combination of Eastwood's imposing persona and Siegel's austere direction. Siegel's interest in the monotony of prisoners' lives provides an astute study of incarceration, which he skillfully develops as the momentum for the escape. *Escape from Alcatraz* was Siegel's last notable film. Eastwood acknowledges Siegel as one of his mentors.

Screenwriter **RICHARD TUGGLE** was a novice when he penned the screenplay for *Escape from Alcatraz*, based on the book by **J. CAMPBELL BRUCE** about the real 1962 Alcatraz escape. Tuttle's initial interest was sparked after taking a tour of the island prison and hearing about the unsolved escape. In 1984, Tuggle worked with Eastwood writing the screenplay and directing *Tightrope*.

Cinematographer BRUCE SURTEES captures the raw chill, foggy light, and tight confinement on Alcatraz from the film's striking opening cellhouse sequence to the cramped shots of Eastwood toiling in his 5' x 7' cell. At twenty-four, Surtees got his first job as a camera operator on Siegel and Eastwood's first collaboration, *Coogan's Bluff* (1968). Three years later, he was the cinematographer on Siegel's *The Beguiled*, starring Eastwood, and on Eastwood's directorial debut, *Play Misty for Me* (both 1971). His films include *Leadbelly* (1976), *Risky Business* (1983), *Beverly Hills Cop* (1984), *Men Don't Leave* (1990), and many television films. Surtees, who received an Oscar nomination for *Lenny* (1974), is the son of the great cinematographer Robert Surtees.

Editor FERRIS WEBSTER was one of Hollywood's top artists, working on MGM films through the '40s and '50s, including *Madame Bovary* (1949), *Father of the Bride* (1950), *The Blackboard Jungle* (1955, Oscar nomination), and *Cat on a Hot Tin Roof* (1958). He received a second Oscar nomination for *The Manchurian Candidate* (1962), directed by John Frankenheimer (*Birdman of Alcatraz*), and again a year later for *The Great Escape* (1963). Webster's last fifteen films were with Clint Eastwood, starting with *Joe Kidd* (1972) and ending with *Honkytonk Man* (1982), after which he retired at age seventy.

Composer JERRY FIELDING is remembered for his bold and creative work. Siegel filmed many scenes in *Escape* with only ambient sounds of prison life and without musical accompaniment. Fielding's subtle score, which underlines the tense story, seems to rumble from beneath the water that surrounds the island, capturing the prison's sense of isolation. A brave anti-McCarthy stance led to Fielding's late start in developing his musical career, but he made an auspicious movie debut on Otto Preminger's *Advise and Consent* (1962). His films include *The Wild Bunch* (1969, Oscar nomination), *Straw Dogs* (1971, Oscar nomination), *Junior Bonner* (1972), *Scorpio* (1973), and *The Gambler* (1974). Fielding and Eastwood worked on three other films together, including *The Outlaw Josey Wales* (Oscar nomination) and *The Enforcer* (both 1976), and *The Gauntlet* (1977). He died a year after scoring *Escape from Alcatraz* (1979) at the age of fifty-eight.

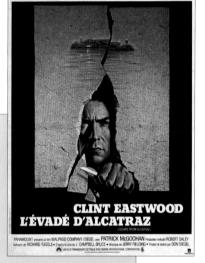

film poster

The illustration for the *Escape from Alcatraz* poster is by acclaimed artist **BIRNEY LETTICK** (1919–1986). Lettick, who received a classical art education, attended Yale University, where he studied with influential artist Joseph Albers and learned anatomy by dissecting cadavers. His talent was recognized early on when he won the prestigious Tiffany Scholarship given to the country's ten most promising art students. Lettick became a top cover illustrator for magazines including *Time*, *Newsweek*, *National Lampoon*, and *National Geographic*, and was involved with many national advertising campaigns. His film posters include *Thunderbolt and Lightfoot* (1974), *Foul Play* (1978), *Heaven Can Wait* (1978), *Star Trek: The Motion Picture* (1979), *Superman: The Movie* (1979), *The Border* (1982), *Paternity* (1981), *Valley Girl* (1983), and *Lost in America* (1985).

Working with Clint Eastwood and designer Bill Gold (who oversaw most of Eastwood's film posters), Lettick developed a deceptively simple illustration, handsomely weaving an image of Alcatraz high on the tombstone-like wall, cleverly conveying the isolation and mystery of the island prison. Lettick's mastery of the portrait is revealed in the detailed rendering of Eastwood's distinctive face. To capture Eastwood's famous features, Gail Lettick, Birney's widow, said her husband worked from sittings with Eastwood as well as photos, and that the actor purchased the original artwork for himself.

MURDER IN THE FIRST

Directed by
MARC ROCCO

WARNER BROTHERS, WOLPER ORGANIZATION,
LE STUDIO CANAL
122 minutes, Color

CAST

Christian Slater	James Stamphill
Kevin Bacon	Henri Young
Gary Oldman	Associate Warden Milton Glenn
Embeth Davidtz	Mary McCasslin
Brad Dourif	Byron Stamphill
William H. Macy	D.A. William McNeil
R. Lee Ermey	Judge Clawson
Stephen Tobolowsky	Mr. Henkin
Mia Kirshner	Adult Rosetta Young
Ben Slack	Jerry Hollihan
Stefan Gierasch	Warden James Humson
Kyra Sedgwick	Blanche, Hooker
Alex Bookston	Alcatraz Doc
Richie Allan	Jury Foreman
Herb Ritts	Mike Kelly
Charles Boswell	Derek Simpson
David Michael Sterling	Rufus McCain
Michael Melvin	Doc Barker

CREATIVE

Producer	Marc Frydman, Mark Wolper
Screenplay	Dan Gordon
Cinematography	Fred Murphy
Editing	Russell Livingstone
Original Music	Buddy Feyne, Christopher Young
Production Design	Kirk M. Petruccelli
Art Direction	Greg J. Grande
Costume Design	Sylvia Vega-Vasquez

CHRISTIAN SLATER   KEVIN BACON   GARY OLDMAN

One was
condemned.

One was
determined.

Two men
whose friendship
gave them the
will to take
on the system...

MURDER
IN THE FIRST

The trial that brought down Alcatraz.

WARNER BROS. PRESENTS
A LE STUDIO CANAL + PRODUCTION IN ASSOCIATION WITH THE WOLPER ORGANIZATION
A FILM BY MARC ROCCO CHRISTIAN SLATER KEVIN BACON
GARY OLDMAN "MURDER IN THE FIRST" EMBETH DAVIDTZ BRAD DOURIF WILLIAM H. MACY R. LEE ERMEY
MUSIC BY CHRISTOPHER YOUNG EDITED BY DEBORAH LEE CASTING BY RUSSELL LIVINGSTONE PRODUCTION DESIGNER KIRK M. PETRUCCELLI DIRECTOR OF PHOTOGRAPHY FRED MURPHY
EXECUTIVE PRODUCERS DAVID L. WOLPER AND MARC ROCCO SCREENPLAY BY DAN GORDON PRODUCED BY MARC FRYDMAN AND MARK WOLPER
DIRECTED BY MARC ROCCO

THE STORY

In the late 1930s, four convicts escape from prison on Alcatraz Island, but are caught clinging to the base of the newly built Golden Gate Bridge. Two men are killed, and two—Henri Young and Rufus McCain—are returned to the prison.

McCain, who had secretly tipped off the warden about the escape, is put back into the general population, while Young is sent to the "hole," one of the below-ground cells in what the prisoners call the "dungeon." These cells are little more than cages: no water, no toilet, no light. Young is confined naked in the dark, like a wild animal; his "baths" consist of having water thrown at him. His food is shoved through a slot. Though official regulations mandate no more than nineteen consecutive days in the hole, Young is kept in there for three years and regularly tortured by Associate Warden Milton Glenn. Since Warden James Humson is rarely at the prison, he knows nothing about Young or his extended punishment.

During one of Warden Humson's reviews of the cell-rotation roster, he notices that a prisoner has been in the hole for three years. He insists that Glenn put the inmate back into the general population. But three years of torture and confinement have left Young a barely functioning, deeply disturbed man. In his first visit to the mess hall, fellow prisoners tell him that McCain was responsible for his confinement. McCain's name reverberates in his head, and, in a highly agitated state, Young attacks and kills McCain. He is charged with murder in the first degree.

A young San Francisco lawyer, James Stamphill, is given his first case: defend Henri Young. Everyone assumes Young is guilty, and the DA wants a quick verdict. When Stamphill reviews Young's file, he reads that at seventeen, he stole $5 from a country store to feed his younger sister. He is caught, but because the store was also a post office, his crime is a federal offense. Sent to Alcatraz, eleven years later he kills Rufus McCain. His brief bio disturbs Stamphill, as it gives no indication of what happened during those eleven years to turn Young into a murderer.

Stamphill visits Young in San Francisco's city jail, where he awaits trial. Young is extremely frightened, curled up on a bed and afraid to speak. Stamphill slowly coaxes him to talk, and learns about Young's torture and years in the hole. When Stamphill goes to the prison and sees the below-ground cells, he is shocked by the barbaric conditions; he decides that, in order to defend his client, he will put Alcatraz on trial for its cruel practices. In his opening statement, Stamphill makes headlines when he calls the prison the "Rock of torture," provoking a backlash against him from the DA's office, the Federal Bureau of Prisons, and the FBI.

When Young testifies, his clearly visible terror convinces the jury that Alcatraz was indeed culpable. Though Young is found "not guilty" of first-degree murder, he must serve three years for involuntary manslaughter—on the Rock. Before Stamphill can file an appeal, Young is found dead in his jail cell. Associate Warden Glenn is brought up on charges of mistreatment and exiled from the penal system. The dungeons of Alcatraz are closed forever.

THE INSIDE SCOOP

Murder in the First is a stylish period film that vividly tells the story of one prisoner's horrifying life on Alcatraz. The film sets up a strong case against Alcatraz, and the scenes in which Young is sadistically tortured by the prison's associate warden—played with spirited malevolence by Gary Oldman—are particularly powerful. In the great tradition of good triumphing over evil, with the odds stacked against him, first-time lawyer Stamphill makes a rousing and heroic defense, and in the nick of time, Henri Young finds the courage to speak and win the case. Before the final credits roll, Alcatraz is brought down, and justice is served.

Murder in the First was one of the biggest film shoots ever undertaken on Alcatraz, and the National Park Service gave Warner Brothers full access to the island so they could tell a more realistic story. The crew spent over two weeks filming on Alcatraz, using the hospital ward for the actor's dressing rooms and repainting sections of the cellblock to resemble the original time period. The filmmakers not only had to use boats and barges to haul their equipment to the island, but in 1994 during filming, the National Park Service welcomed thousands of visitors to Alcatraz daily, adding the challenging task of shooting while hundreds of onlookers tried to get a glimpse of the stars. The film opens with the statement, "This film is inspired by a true story," an announcement that leads the audience to accept the film as a reliable account of events. Unfortunately, it is a combination of pure fabrication and semi-factual information, telling a story that dramatically obscures the truth about both Henri Young and Alcatraz—for example, Henri Young was not an orphan, and he never stole to feed his sister; that aspect of the story is loosely based on the experience of Alcatraz convict Joseph Bowers, who, with an accomplice, was caught stealing $16.67 from a store that doubled as a post office.

THE REAL HENRI YOUNG

Henri Young was born on June 20, 1911, the second of four children of Helen and David Young. The family was poor and his parents divorced when Henri was fourteen. His mother's second marriage, to a man with six children, was difficult for Henri, and he left home at nineteen.

Young began his criminal career when he and friend Elmer Webb robbed and then tied up a man (who almost died before he was rescued). Young was apprehended, served jail time, and four months later was convicted of armed burglary and sent to Montana State Prison for fifteen months.

After his release he was caught for another crime, sentenced to one to ten years, and sent to Walla Walla State Prison in Washington. Released the same year, he was free only a month before he committed an armed bank robbery, in which kidnapping and car-jacking may have been involved. On November 2, 1934, Young and two accomplices robbed a bank at gunpoint, but their getaway car promptly got a flat tire and they were immediately apprehended. Young received two twenty-year sentences. Incarcerated at USP McNeil Island (which is now a state correctional facility), he quickly became a problem prisoner. McNeil Island's associate warden, E.B. Swope (who would later become warden of Alcatraz) called Young "the worst and most dangerous criminal with whom I've ever dealt," stating for the record on June, 1, 1935, "He is vicious, unscrupulous, and is a fomenter of trouble, but still has enough ingenuity to keep undercover."

Young was sent to Alcatraz for maximum security. He was considered highly unstable, alert, shrewd, definitely capable of long-term planning, and as having "extreme personality disorganization." Young probably suffered from paranoid schizophrenia. The term appears many times in his records, and his behavior seemed consistent with that diagnosis.

On the Rock, Young was the recipient of thirty-four disciplinary reports, including reprimands for fist-fights, joining strikes, agitating others, attempting to stab a prisoner, flushing a homemade knife down the toilet, concealing a brass dagger fashioned from a toilet plunger hidden in his mattress, setting fire in his cell, flooding his cell, attempting to escape, and finally, murder.

According to testimony given by Warden Johnston during Young's subsequent trial, he was sent to lower isolation on at least three occasions for serious violations. "Lower isolation" consisted of eight cells located beneath the cellhouse floor. Part of the original Citadel, or the Civil War-era defensive barracks, these were primitive brick rooms (once used by the army for storage) with no running water or furnishings. Prisoners were served basic meals, given a bucket for waste (which was removed once or twice a day), and provided with water in a basin. Their use was strictly regulated by guidelines set by Warden Johnston, known as one of the leading advocates of prisoner rights and rehabilitation.

Young's big trouble began on January 13, 1939, when he, "Doc" Barker, Dale Stamphill, Rufus McCain, and William Martin attempted to escape from five solitary confinement cells in D Block. Rumors circulated that McCain was not able to swim and wanted to back out just as they reached the water's edge. "Doc" Barker was killed, Dale Stamphill was injured, and the others were brought back and put in solitary confinement cells located on the upper tiers of cellblocks A and D. These cells were equipped with toilets, sinks, a mattress, and blankets.

Young may well have blamed McCain for the failure of the 1939 escape attempt, but the film's depiction of Young striking out in a delusional fit after three years in the hole is misleading. Young and McCain were both violent career criminals who continually committed serious infractions. Young was released from solitary (a cell on the top floor of A Block) twenty-three months after the escape attempt. Both men were in the general population and working in the Model Shop building when on December 3, 1940, Young left his place of work in the Model Shop; went downstairs to the second floor; entered the tailor shop; and, in cold blood, fatally stabbed Rufus McCain.

The movie depicts Young's personality disintegration as a result of solitary confinement on Alcatraz. At the famous 1941 trial, lawyers made headline news, declaring that Young was not a cold-blooded killer, but a victim of Alcatraz's brutal conditions. The defense called more than twenty inmate witnesses, all of whom described the terrible abuse they suffered on Alcatraz.

Young claimed that Associate Warden Miller abused him, including knocking his teeth out, but these allegations were proved unfounded when dental records showed that only one tooth was extracted, and that was at Young's request. Associate Warden Miller testified he never abused Young, and Warden Johnston vehemently rejected Young and the other cons' claims. However, the defense attorney's arguments were compelling and the jury, much to Judge Roche's dismay, found Young to be a victim and delivered a verdict of involuntary manslaughter.Young received only a three-year sentence, which irritated some prisoners, either because they had liked McCain, or because they felt that such a short sentence implied that their lives were worth only three years of incarceration.

After the trial, Young fell into further personality disintegration. He adopted the Catholic faith, and amazingly, confessed to a murder no one knew about. He detailed the killing in a letter to the Washington state prosecuting attorney, and when these details matched those of a previously unsolved crime, they tried and convicted him for it. He also had a number of troubling symptoms, including hearing voices, becoming catatonic, and exhibiting a distrust of psychiatrists (calling them Jesuits in civilian clothing).

On June 20, 1948, his 37th birthday, Young stripped naked and stood in his cell refusing to eat. He was transferred to the prison hospital with symptoms of catatonic schizophrenia. He stared, postured, and didn't talk to staff members, though he did talk to other cons. He was transferred to Springfield on September 13, 1948, appearing catatonic, "but was observed talking rationally to other inmates." After "sodium amytal interviews," he was diagnosed as a schizophrenic of the paranoid type. Young was paroled out of the federal prison on December 9, 1954, and sent under guard to Walla Walla State Prison for life for "murder in the first degree" for the 1933 murder to which he'd confessed. In 1972, at the age of sixty-one, Young was paroled from the state prison at Walla Walla, but violated parole in 1973 by not reporting in to his parole officer. He is still wanted by the State of Washington.

INSIDE CELLHOUSE, "BROADWAY," LOOKING NORTH TOWARD DINING ROOM

the studio: WARNER BROTHERS

In the 1980s and '90s, as mergers began to dominate the business world, Warner Brothers was at the center of some of the biggest in history. In 1989, Time Inc. paid $14 billion in cash and securities to take over Warner Communications. Now called Time Warner Inc., it became one of the world's media giants. They increased their standing in 1994 with the takeover of Turner Broadcasting for in excess of $7 billion. In 2000, AOL bought Time Warner for over $160 billion in shares at the height of the dot-com boom, a deal that was supposed to bridge the gap between traditional media and new technologies, but which became a financial disaster when the dot-com bubble burst. Throughout these corporate deals, the film division continued to produce hits including *Batman* (and its sequels, 1989–1995), *Driving Miss Daisy* (1989), *Unforgiven* (1992), *The Fugitive* (1993), and in the early 21st century, the phenomenal *"Harry Potter"* and *"Lord of the Rings"* series. Amongst these giants, *Murder in the First* made a slim showing, earning just over $17 million at the box office. *Murder in the First* was co-produced by Le Studio Canal and the Wolper Organization.

ALCATRAZ: REEL TO REAL

Although the movie took place in the late 1930s, exterior shots of Alcatraz show the burned-out shell of the warden's house. The warden's house on Alcatraz didn't burn until 1970, seven years after it was closed as a prison, during the occupation of the island by Native American activists.

Money paid to the NPS for use of the island by the movie company was used to help finish restoration of the dock guard tower ($40,000 worth of labor was supplied by Federal Bureau of Prisons inmates from FCI Dublin, CA.) Also donated were hospital "rule" signs and benches in the mess hall. A 1941 Chevy stake-bed truck, similar to one actually used on Alcatraz, was also donated, though scenes in which it appeared were ultimately cut from the film.

Christian Slater's character's name, James Stamphill, is taken from two factual sources. "James" was James Macinnis, one of Young's lawyers, and "Stamphill" was Dale Stamphill, an Alcatraz inmate who attempted to escape with Young. (Young's other lawyer was Sol Abrams.)

The film states that the Alcatraz warden did not live on Alcatraz and simultaneously managed three prisons: Alcatraz, and state prisons at San Quentin and Folsom. In fact, Alcatraz's warden lived on the island and managed only Alcatraz; no warden has ever been simultaneously in charge of both a federal and a state prison.

When Alcatraz was first opened as a federal prison, there were no solitary confinement cells. The only place to isolate a prisoner was in the demolished Citadel's below-ground storage rooms, which had been retained for the prison's use.

**"Henri, I have a job to do at Alcatraz.
Do you know what that is?
TO PROTECT YOU FROM YOURSELF."**

Associate Warden Glenn, *Murder in the First*

STARRING

KEVIN BACON (Henri Young) delivers a striking portrayal as the tortured prisoner, earning a Screen Actors Guild nomination. Bacon's first film was a small part in the hit comedy *Animal House* (1978), followed by a featured role in the horror film *Friday the 13th* (1980). But it was Barry Levinson's breakout movie *Diner* (1982), about five college-age friends in the late '50s, that got Bacon noticed. He followed with the dance sensation *Footloose* (1984) and became a teen heartthrob. Bacon continues to be a prolific and resourceful actor, willing to take risks even where his characters are unsympathetic. His films include *JFK* (1991), *Apollo 13* (1995), *Sleepers* (1996), *Hollowman* (2000), *Mystic River* (2003 directed by Clint Eastwood), *The Woodsman* (2004), and *Where the Truth Lies* (2005).

CHRISTIAN SLATER (James Stamphill) made his screen debut at age twelve in the 1981 television version of *Sherlock Holmes*, starring Frank Langella. At seventeen, he was cast opposite Sean Connery in *The Name of the Rose* (1986). His other films include *Tucker: The Man and His Dreams* (1988), directed by Francis Ford Coppola; *Heathers* (1989); *Robin Hood: Prince of Thieves* (1991); *Interview with a Vampire* (1994); *The Contender* (2000); and *The Deal* (2005).

GARY OLDMAN (Milton Glenn) is known for tackling difficult roles, from Sid Vicious (*Sid and Nancy*, 1986) and Joe Orton (*Prick up Your Ears*, 1987) to Lee Harvey Oswald (*JFK*, 1991) and Ludwig von Beethoven (*Immortal Beloved*, 1994). Oldman, who is wonderfully convincing as a sadistic prison official in *Murder in the First*, has played his share of villains, notably in *Dracula* (1992), *Lost in Space* and *The Fifth Element* (both 1997), *Air Force One* (1998), and *The Contender* (2000). He has had a recurring role in the *"Harry Potter"* film series (1994–2004) as Sirius Black.

BRAD DOURIF (Byron Stamphill) received an Oscar nomination when he was twenty-five for his second film, *One Flew Over the Cuckoo's Nest* (1975). He gave memorable performances in *Wise Blood* (1979), *Ragtime* (1981), *Mississippi Burning* (1988), *Final Judgment* (1992), and in *The Lord of the Rings: The Two Towers* (2002). He is also the menacing voice of the murderous doll in the *Chucky* horror film series.

EMBETH DAVIDTZ (Mary McCasslin) first came to the public's attention for her tragic portrayal of Helen Hirsch, a Jewish maid terrorized by an SS officer (Ralph Fiennes) in Steven Spielberg's *Schindler's List* (1993). Her films include *Gingerbread Man* (1998), *Bicentennial Man* (1999), and *The Emperor's Club* (2002).

WILLIAM H. MACY (DA William McNeil) is a popular film and television actor, producer, and writer who has been cast in both supporting and lead roles. He has had a long association with director and playwright David Mamet, appearing in *House of Games* (1987), *Things Change* (1988), *Homicide* (1991), *Oleanna* (1994), and *State and Main* (2000). Macy has also worked in movies as varied as *Boogie Nights* (1997), *Pleasantville* (1998), *Magnolia* (1999), *The Cooler* (2003), and *Seabiscuit* (2003). In 1996, Macy received an Oscar nomination for his role as an unlikely and exasperated murderer in the hit film *Fargo*. He won two Emmy awards in 2003 for writing and acting in *Door to Door*. In 2005 he produced the film *Transamerica*, starring his wife Felicity Huffman.

BEHIND THE SCENES

Director **MARC ROCCO** began his career at twenty-five, writing, directing, and producing his first film, *Scenes from the Goldmine* (1987). He did it again on his next two films, *Dream a Little Dream* (1989), with a cast that included Jason Robards, Piper Laurie, and Harry Dean Stanton; and *Where the Day Takes You* (1992), with Laura San Giacomo, Dermot Mulroney, Sean Astin, and Will Smith. His fourth directorial effort was *Murder in the First*, with another cast of popular actors.

Screenwriter DAN GORDON is known for his action/adventure films and television shows. His film credits include *Passenger 57* (1992), *Wyatt Earp* (1994), *The Assignment* (1997), and *The Hurricane* (1999). Gordon's dialogue suits the film's dramatic intentions, as in these closing remarks from James Stamphill, "Unlike many men who lived long after, Henri Young did not die in vain. In the end he was not afraid. He lived and he died in triumph. If only we could all do that."

Cinematographer FRED MURPHY creates a beautiful noir atmosphere for *Murder in the First*, making the most of every scene (sometimes too much) by shooting from unusual angles (including below someone reading a newspaper), with multiple 360-degree and overhead shots that give the viewer an eyeful. Murphy's work includes the striking Western *Heartland* (1980), the B horror film *Q* (1982), John Huston's elegant *The Dead* (1987), and *Secret Window* (2004).

Production Designer KURT M. PETRUCCELLI, Art Director MICHAEL RIZZO, and **Set Decorator GREG J. GRANDE** create a impressive palette for the film, including the intolerably claustrophobic cell in which Young is confined and an elegant courtroom, richly appointed with stained glass windows, wrought-iron metal work, and dark wood paneling. Petruccelli's films include *Blade* (1998), *The Patriot* (2000), and the *"Lara Croft/Tomb Raider"* series (2001, 2003). Rizzo's work includes *My Cousin Vinny* (1992), the Alcatraz-related *So I Married an Axe Murderer* (1993), and *Vanilla Sky* (2001). Grande has worked in television as well on the feature film *Blade* (1998).

film poster

The poster for *Murder in the First* beautifully reflects the film's dark palette and overall rich aesthetic. The movie poster's tagline reads, "One was condemned. One was determined. Two men, whose friendship gave them the will to take on the system..." These words accurately reflect the movie, though the truth is something quite different.

The handsome period-looking photographs of stars Christian Slater and Kevin Bacon, along with the names of all three leads, are the focus of the poster. The three young and popular actors are the film's major marketing tools. Alcatraz is secondary, appearing below the title: "The trial that brought down Alcatraz."

METAL SHOP, INDUSTRIES BUILDING—*IN REAL LIFE, INMATE HENRI YOUNG MURDERED RUFUS McCAIN HERE.*

THE ROCK

Directed by
MICHAEL BAY

HOLLYWOOD PICTURES/
A DON SIMPSON AND
JERRY BRUCKHEIMER PRODUCTION
136 minutes, Color

CAST

Sean Connery	John Patrick Mason
Nicolas Cage	Stanley Goodspeed
Ed Harris	Brigadier General Hummel
David Morse	Major Tom Baxter
John Spencer	FBI Director James Womack
William Forsythe	Special Agent Ernest Paxton
John C. McGinley	Captain Hendrix
Tony Todd	Captain Darrow
Bokeem Woodbine	Sergeant Crisp
Danny Nucci	Lieutenant Shepard
Claire Forlani	Jade Angelou
Vanessa Marcil	Carla Pestalozzi
Gregory Sporleder	Captain Frey
Jim Maniaci	Private Scarpetti
Steve Harris	Private McCoy

CREATIVE

Executive Producer	William Stuart, Sean Connery, Louis A. Stroller
Producer	Don Simpson, Jerry Bruckheimer
Story	David Weisberg, Douglas S. Cook
Screenplay	David Weisberg, Douglas S. Cook, Mark Rosner
Cinematography	John Schwartzman
Editing	Richard Francis-Bruce
Production Design	Michael White
Music	Nick Glennie-Smith, Hans Zimmer
Costumes	Bobbie Read
Special Effects	Michael Meinardus
Special Effects Make-up	Tony Gardner
Technical Advisor	Harry Humphries

On a rainy night, decorated Brigadier General Francis X. Hummel leads a renegade team of ex-Navy Seals in an ambush of a military compound, where they steal six VX missiles carrying payloads of toxic nerve gas.

Later, on Alcatraz, Ranger Bob is leading a tour when Hummel and his team take over the island, locking visitors and rangers alike in the old cells. After helicopters carrying the stolen VX missiles and more troops land on the island. Hummel contacts the Pentagon and demands $100 million for the families of Marines who died in covert actions, their loss unacknowledged and their families denied death benefits. He threatens the destruction of San Francisco if the money is not in the specified account at the end of 48 hours.

The FBI brings in Stanley Goodspeed, their best chemical weapons expert, and the only man who has ever escaped from the Rock, John Patrick Mason. The FBI has kept Mason, a British citizen, imprisoned and incommunicado for thirty years. He agrees to help them when he is offered his freedom as a reward.

A small team—marines, Goodspeed, and Mason—is deployed, equipped with scuba gear. They enter the San Francisco Bay just beyond the Alcatraz shoreline and reach the island through a large underwater pipe. Led by Mason, they head through a series of tunnels, and come up under the prison's shower room. The marines ascend, leaving Goodspeed and Mason below. Hummel's men are waiting, and acting against his orders, they kill the entire group. Goodspeed and Mason race from the scene, escape a bomb attack, and navigate through the underground tunnels. In the process, they kill off attackers and find and defuse three of the six rockets. Meanwhile, the Pentagon is planning to drop a new thermal-plasma bomb on the island, which will destroy the VX poison gas and kill everyone on Alcatraz.

Through island loudspeakers, Hummel threatens to kill a hostage if Goodspeed and Mason don't give up. Mason surrenders, but Goodspeed continues hunting down the missiles. After destroying one more weapon, Goodspeed is captured and tossed in a cell next to Mason. As Goodspeed laments their situation, Mason deftly unlocks their cell doors, and they resume their search for the remaining missiles.

The 48-hour time limit is running out, and Hummel gives the OK to fire off a rocket. It heads toward Candlestick Park's packed stadium, but at the last minute, Hummel reprograms its course and sends it out to sea. His men, furious, take over. Hummel is shot, but with his dying breath tells Goodspeed where the remaining rockets are. The two surviving members of Hummel's team go after Goodspeed and Mason to stop them from destroying the missiles. Unaware of what is taking place on Alcatraz, the president of the United States decides to bomb the island in order to save San Francisco. Goodspeed and Mason destroy the last two rockets, but the government's plasma bombs are on their way, unless Goodspeed can send the all-clear signal in time.

VIEW OF SAN FRANCISCO FROM INDUSTRIES BUILDING

THE INSIDE SCOOP

The Rock was the biggest film ever made on Alcatraz. It catapulted the island prison into the realm of big budget, big action, and big box-office movies. The film cost an estimated $75 million, had opening-day receipts totaling $25 million, and a total worldwide gross to date of $325 million; video rentals added another $75 million. *The Rock* was Disney's top-grossing film of the year; was named *"Favorite Movie of the Year"* by the National Association of Theater Owners (NATO); and upon its release, set the video rental market record as the most-ordered film in history. Created by über-producers Jerry Bruckheimer and Don Simpson, and with an all-star cast headed by Sean Connery, Nicolas Cage, and Ed Harris, *The Rock* introduced Alcatraz to a new generation of movie-goers.

The movie's fast pace, exploding bombs, terrifying chemical weapons, and roller-coaster thrills are combined with a wonderfully wry script, deft editing, exciting special effects, and hilarious moments courtesy of Connery and Cage. Connery's ever-suave action hero persona perfectly suits his role as the only man in the world who can save San Francisco from destruction. He becomes Cage's mentor, and they make a great team, sparring verbally as they battle their way through a multitude of harrowing, totally fictitious, and wildly courageous moments.

the studio: WALT DISNEY AND HOLLYWOOD PICTURES

Hollywood Pictures was created in 1989, as the second production subsidiary of the famed Walt Disney Studios (following the successful Touchstone Pictures, formed in the early '80s). The intention of these divisions was to enable the studio to develop films for an adult audience. Hollywood Pictures scored their first success with *The Hand That Rocks the Cradle* (1992), and went on to release *The Joy Luck Club* (1993), *The Santa Clause* (1994), and *The Sixth Sense* (1999). Don Simpson and Jerry Bruckheimer found *The Rock* while working on *Crimson Tide* (1995), also for Hollywood Pictures.

Producers **JERRY BRUCKHEIMER** and the late **DON SIMPSON** began their prolific fourteen-year partnership in 1983 with the hit film *Flashdance*. Their work has been honored by fifteen Academy Award nominations, two Oscars, four Grammys, Golden Globes, and other accolades. Their worldwide gross is in the billions of dollars, making their work among the most commercially popular of all time. Bruckheimer and Simpson's films, notable for their big stars and big action, include *Beverly Hills Cop* (1984), *Top Gun* (1986), *Bad Boys* (1995), and *Dangerous Minds* (1995). Simpson died on January 19, 1996, six months before *The Rock* opened, but Bruckheimer has gone on to produce many successful television shows and films, including *CSI* (TV 2000) and its spin-offs, *The Amazing Race* (TV 2001) reality series, *Con Air* (1997), *Pirates of the Caribbean: The Curse of the Black Pearl* (2003), and *National Treasure* (2004).

BIG MOVIE, BIG PREMIERE

Hollywood Pictures and Buena Vista premiered *The Rock* at a special invitation-only screening on Alcatraz Island on June 3, 1996, four days before its national release. A complete theater, taking a week to construct, was built in the prison's recreation yard. The dining hall was carpeted for a sit-down dinner with cocktails and tours of the prison. The elite of Hollywood were on hand for this once-in-a-lifetime event that was broadcast on E-TV. One of the first large-scale events to take place after hours on Alcatraz, its success contributed to NPS acceptance of the Alcatraz "Night Tour," evening programs offering historical interpretation of Alcatraz as a Civil War defensive garrison, a federal penitentiary, and the site of the 1969–71 Native American occupation. (Fees collected from the evening programs help support restoration projects on the island.)

FILMING ON THE ROCK

The Rock was shot in almost every area on the island, both interior and exterior, and filming on Alcatraz was challenging. "It's a nightmare shooting out there", said Bay, "But, Alcatraz is really cool. It's a mystical place, very eerie." The crew contended with the island's variable weather, which could go from sunny to cloudy to foggy within a single hour, playing havoc with a meticulously prepared shoot. And, as though the weather weren't enough, the island is inhabited by a large and vociferous gull population, which, unlike the island's human visitors, could not be induced to cooperate with the promise of a movie star's autograph. Alcatraz is also an historic landmark, and unlike damage to newer buildings, which a film company can repair, Alcatraz's many old and unique structures required particular care.

To accommodate a major film production, trailers and trucks filled with movie equipment were loaded onto barges, shipped across San Francisco Bay, and lifted off by a gigantic 125-ton crane onto the island. Food and supplies (including water) also had to be brought to the island. Filmmakers worked with National Park Service staff to protect the bird population (nesting season closes part of the island to public visitation each year) and accommodate concerns involving the thousands of visitors who tour the island daily. Since Alcatraz had not been used as a federal penitentiary for over thirty years, many of the buildings were in disrepair, and the studio also worked with the NPS on upgrades and removal of toxic paint.

The historic "shutdown" of the federal government between November 14 and November 20, 1995, provided the movie-makers with a rare opportunity. Reaching a partisan budget impasse, the government partially suspended operation, at a cost of close to $800 million. Among other things, two million visitors were turned away from the country's national parks. *The Rock* reaped some unexpected rewards, however, as its crew filmed without interruption from visitors. They used the opportunity to take wide-angle daytime shots, which were normally impossible.

At first, the plan was to film the tunnel sequences in the small tunnels built during the Civil War to transport men and supplies from one side of the island to the other. This idea was abandoned when the filmmakers found that the tunnels were filled with asbestos. Instead, a thirty-foot tank once used for swimming star Esther Williams was a stand-in for the island's "tunnels." Equipped with a removable floor, the tank was used by the production design team, who spent four months creating the underwater world of Alcatraz. According to production designer Michael White, "We built them to interconnect, like a real tunnel system [though nothing like it is actually on Alcatraz]. Although we built in flying walls, we made the tunnels as long and realistic as possible so that Michael [Bay] could film continuously and follow the actors as they traveled through the maze of sewer and railway systems." To create a realistic background for the military maneuvers, ex-Navy Seal Harry Humphries was brought in. Humphries put the cast through rigorous training, and assisted in upgrading the attacks and language to make them more militaristic. In fact, Humphries secured the services of a few actual Navy Seals to be in the film.

Director Michael Bay

"At first we thought maybe we'd double Alcatraz on stage, but then I did a location scout up there and when I saw it, I knew we had to shoot there. One side of the island looks like France and Europe, and another looks like a hard-core prison, and another is just beautiful rocky bluffs. It's got all these looks you can't double."

Producer Jerry Bruckheimer

"It draws people in. In every picture that's been made about Alcatraz, it never ceases to fascinate audiences. It always elicits a strong reaction."

Actor Sean Connery

"The story is indigenous to Alcatraz. The whole idea of the escape we perform, finding our way back, where the FBI sets up headquarters, every main feature is tied to Alcatraz. That's why it's called *The Rock*."

"Alcatraz is quite impressive. It changed every day. We had one sequence where we filmed in the tower where the fog came in. It looks unreal on film, just like a special effect that would cost zillions of dollars."

Actor Ed Harris

"The place has its ghosts, but it was great to shoot out there because Alcatraz has its own atmosphere and its own feeling of isolation. With the fog, wind and dampness, it gave a sense of reality."

STARRING

SEAN CONNERY (Patrick Mason) is perfect as a notorious ex-Alcatraz inmate, an extraordinary escape artist, a top-secret prisoner, and—what else—a British spy. As the movie's action hero and its "senior" star (he was sixty-six at the time), Connery projects a suave persona and is, as usual, the calm in the storm of bombs and guns that surrounds him. Connery's presence adds significant stature to the film, and it became his biggest single motion-picture release.

Connery worked at a variety of jobs before taking an uncredited film role at age twenty-five in *Lilacs in Spring* (1955). Seven years and twenty film and television shows later came his star-making turn as Agent 007, James Bond, in *Dr. No* (1962). He followed with *From Russia with Love* (1962), *Goldfinger* (1964), *Thunderball* (1965), *You Only Live Twice* (1967), and *Diamonds are Forever* (1971), before deciding to give up his signature Astin Martin. It took twelve years to lure him back for one last Bond picture, the aptly named, *Never Say Never Again* (1983). The entire Bond series continues to be the most successful ever produced, and made Sean Connery an international movie star and screen heartthrob. Connery's striking looks, Scottish brogue, and personal magnetism put him in the same league as Clark Gable or Cary Grant (who was, in fact, initially offered the role of James Bond and turned it down because he didn't want to commit to a series). Connery's confidence, strength, intelligence, and charm (fully apparent in *The Rock*), are all the more appealing because he casually underplays them.

Connery's many fine films include *Marnie* (1964), *A Fine Madness* (1966), *The Anderson Tapes* (1971), *Murder on the Orient Express* (1974), *The Man Who Would Be King* (1976), *Highlander* (1986), *The Name of the Rose* (1986), *The Hunt for Red October* (1990), *Finding Forester* (2000), and *The League of Extraordinary Gentlemen* (2003). He was well cast as the father of the daring archeologist played by Harrison Ford in *Indiana Jones and the Last Crusade* (1989). Connery received an Academy Award for his performance as Irish cop Jim Malone, assisting Eliot Ness in bringing down Al Capone (who, in real life, spent four years on Alcatraz, 1934 to 1939) in Brian DePalma's *The Untouchables* (1986).

NICOLAS CAGE (Stanley Goodspeed) gives a wonderful performance in *The Rock*, playing a chemical weapons expert with no field experience trying to remain calm in the face of one catastrophe after another. *The Rock* was Cage's first action picture, which he followed with another action picture, *Con Air* (1997), again produced by Jerry Bruckheimer for Touchstone Pictures. Cage, who has the rare ability to be both insecure and strong at the same time, began his film career at eighteen, billed as Nicolas Coppola (nephew of legendary director Francis Ford Coppola) in the teenage hit *Fast Times at Ridgemont High* (1982). His popularity grew through films in which he co-starred with other top young actors, including *Valley Girl* and *Rumble Fish* (both 1983), and *Racing with the Moon* and *Birdy* (both 1984).

Cage's unique flair for comedy was used to great effect in *Peggy Sue Got Married* (1986), and *Raising Arizona* and *Moonstruck* (both 1987). In *Leaving Las Vegas* (1995), Cage gave a striking portrayal of a man in a downward spiral, determined to drink himself to death, and was awarded an Oscar for his work. Cage received an Oscar nomination for his hilarious performance as twin brothers in *Adaptation (2002)*, and returned as an action hero in Jerry Bruckheimer's hit, *National Treasure* (2004).

ED HARRIS (Brig. Gen. Francis X. Hummel) is a commanding presence in *The Rock*, a war hero driven to madness by the US government's heartless treatment of his fallen comrades. He is at the center of the movie's storyline, orchestrating a precise military theft of chemical weapons and hijacking Alcatraz Island. Throughout, he is both terrifying and sympathetic: an honorable man committing outrageous acts for a just cause. Harris is well known for his powerful work in films including *The Right Stuff* (1983), *Places in the Heart* (1984), *Sweet Dreams* (1985), *Glengarry Glenn Ross* (1992), and *A Beautiful Mind* (2001). He has received numerous acting awards, including four Oscar nominations for *Apollo 13* (1995), *The Truman Show* (1998), *Pollock* (2000), and *The Hours* (2002).

JOHN SPENCER (FBI Director Womack) garnered public attention for his role as Chief of Staff Leo McGarry in the acclaimed television drama, *The West Wing* (premiered 1999). Spencer seems right at home in *The Rock*, portraying the hard-nosed head of the FBI squaring off with other government officials. Spencer's acting career started at eighteen with his role as "Henry Anderson" on the popular *Patty Duke* television series (1964–1965). His feature film work includes *Black Rain* (1989), *Presumed Innocent* (1990), and *The Negotiator* (1998).

DAVID MORSE (Major Tom Baxter) delivers a heartfelt performance as Ed Harris's right-hand man who takes over Alcatraz, though this was not Morse's first "assault" on the island. In 1987, he played Marvin Hubbard in the television movie, *Six Against the Rock*, a film that recreated the *Battle of '46*, a foiled escape attempt by a group of inmates who overpowered guards, captured weapons, and closed down the prison. The siege ended with guards and convicts killed. Morse's film work includes *Inside Moves* (1980), *The Indian Runner* (1991), *The Crossing Guard* (1995), *Contact* (1997), *The Green Mile* (1999), and *Dancer in the Dark* (2000).

WILLIAM FORSYTHE's (FBI Special Agent Ernest Paxton) first connection to *The Rock* was made when he played mobster Al Capone in the television series *The Untouchables* (1993). Forsythe's tough-guy looks have allowed him to play both sides of the law in *Once Upon a Time in America* (1984), *Raising Arizona* (1987), *Dick Tracy* (1990), *Giotti* (1996 TV), and *The Librarians* (2004).

"WELCOME TO THE ROCK"

The line "Welcome to the Rock," delivered by Sean Connery as he leads a team onto Alcatraz, comes from two sources. At the end of Clint Eastwood's dramatic induction process in *Escape from Alcatraz* (1979), a guard says, "Welcome to Alcatraz" and then slams the cell door shut as a wave of thunder reverberates through the cellhouse. The filmmakers were also inspired by Bob Ben-Rajab, a former employee of the Golden Gate National Parks Conservancy (the nonprofit organization that supports the Golden Gate National Parks, including Alcatraz). For many years, to their utter delight, thousands of visitors (and *The Rock* filmmakers) were greeted by Bob as they departed boats and stepped onto Alcatraz Island, his robust voice booming the now-familiar line, "Welcome to the Rock, plan your escape."

According to Ben-Rajab, the filmmakers actually filmed him saying his famous announcement for inclusion in the film's sequence that shows visitors heading to the Sally Port, but as is often the case, his part ended up on the cutting room floor.

DOCK, LOOKING TOWARD SALLY PORT

"If we receive launch authority, your mission is to complete thermal destruction of Alcatraz Island."

US Air Force Commander, *The Rock*

BEHIND THE SCENES

Director MICHAEL BAY spent his early career working in advertising and music videos, winning numerous awards and accolades. His first feature film was the hugely successful action comedy *Bad Boys* (1995), starring Will Smith and Martin Lawrence. He followed with *The Rock*, establishing himself as a premier action director. Bay's next two films were, *Armageddon* (1998) and *Pearl Harbor* (2001). Known for spectacular visuals and box-office results, Bay sets a fast pace in *The Rock*, mixing chase scenes and terrifying action sequences with comedy, even throwing in a roller coaster ride in a subterranean mine. It's over the top, completely unbelievable, and very entertaining. Bay directed *Bad Boys II* (2003) and *The Island* (2005).

Story and screenwriters DAVID WEISBERG and **DOUGLAS S. COOK** created a potent storyline about a decorated general who feels so betrayed by his government that he takes desperate measures to rectify the situation. Weisberg, Cook, and screenwriter Mark Rosner keep the dialogue easy and fun, especially geared for the comic skills of Connery and Cage. There were three uncredited screenwriters for *The Rock*: Quentin Tarantino, Jonathan Hensleigh, and Aaron Sorkin.

Cinematographer JOHN SCHWARTZMAN creates a visual feast in *The Rock*, from the opening sequence—a rainy-day visit to a gravesite—to the wild action scenes in the fictitious bowels of Alcatraz. Schwartzman's films include *Benny & Joon* (1993), *Armageddon* (1998), *Pearl Harbor* (2001), and *Seabiscuit* (2003). He received an Oscar nomination and won the American Society of Cinematographer's (ASC) Award for *Seabiscuit*, as well as an ASC nomination for *Pearl Harbor*.

Editor RICHARD FRANCIS-BRUCE meant to follow in his cinematographer-father Jack Bruce's footsteps, but took an editing job when it was available and has since become one of the outstanding craftsmen in his field. Francis-Bruce's sharp editing sets an exciting pace in *The Rock*. The early theft of chemical weapons blasts onto the screen, each cut forcing us further toward the deadly bombs. A roller-coaster sequence in the Alcatraz tunnel speeds along at a frantic pace, taking us along on the hair-raising ride. Francis-Bruce received Oscar nominations for *The Shawshank Redemption* (1994), *Se7en* (1995), and *Air Force One* (1997).

Composer NICK GLENNIE-SMITH's original music score perfectly matched the action of the film, building suspense that carries us from one exciting moment to the next. Glennie-Smith wrote original music for *The Man in the Iron Mask* (1998), *Highlander: Endgame* (2000), *We Were Soldiers* (2002), and *Ella Enchanted* (2004). He has worked for some of the biggest names in the music industry, including Tina Turner, Paul McCartney, and Phil Collins.

Production designer MICHAEL WHITE, Art Director EDWARD T. McAVOY, and **Set Decorator ROSEMARY BRANDENBURG** combined their talents to create a mysterious world of decaying underground tunnels purportedly deep below Alcatraz.

Their talent and magic—which included creating a mineshaft complete with roller coaster-like track—give us the remarkable feeling that we are actually under the prison. A large lighthouse landing was created as the setting for the climactic confrontation over the explosive chemical weapons.

Special Effects Coordinator MICHAEL MEINARDUS masterfully brings the dynamic action to life through pyrotechnic wizardry, sending fireballs soaring through subterranean tunnels right toward the film's heroes and setting the audience on the edge of their seats. Meinardus's films include *Ghost* (1990), *Twister* (1996), *Austin Powers: The Spy Who Shagged Me* (1999), and *Starsky & Hutch* (2004).

Special Effects Make-up Artist TONY GARDNER creates the horrific facial deterioration caused by exposure to the chemical weapons in the film's hair-raising opening sequence. In the scene, one of Ed Harris's men is caught in the weapon vault when a chemical explosive is accidentally broken. We watch in terror and fascination as the gas eats away his features. Gardner's films include *The Return of the Living Dead* (1985), *The Blob* (1988), *The Addams Family* (1991), and *Adaptation* (2002). Gardner was investigated by the Arizona State Police and Missing Persons bureau for effects he created for *Three Kings* (1999); the scene showed a bullet traveling through a soldier's body, and authorities thought that the bullet had been fired through a real human.

film poster

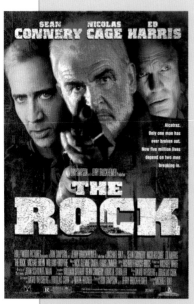

The striking poster for *The Rock* plays off the box-office potential of stars Connery, Cage, and Harris, emblazoning their faces and names across the sheet. The dynamic typeface, made to look like corroding concrete, with an embedded illustration of Alcatraz is outstanding. The creative director for the poster was Oren Aviv, who also wrote the story and was executive producer for *Rocket Man* (1997) and *National Treasure* (2004). Dan Chapman and Diane Reynolds were the art directors, and the finish was executed by Steve Nuchols. Famed photographer **HERB RITTS**, known for his fashion, celebrity, and art images, took the photographs of the stars. A native of Los Angeles, Ritts got started when casual photographs he took of Jon Voight and Ricky Schroeder on the set of *The Champ* (1979) were picked up by *Newsweek* magazine. In 1980, his photographs of a young Richard Gere at a gas station (taken while they were having a tire fixed on a desert drive) helped launch both men's careers.

ALCATRAZ ISLAND

Mason: **"I was just thinking how wonderful it was when the inmates weren't allowed to talk in here."**

Goodspeed: **"Not allowed to talk? How'd you do it?"**

Mason: **"Nurtured the hope that there was hope. That one day I'd breathe free air, perhaps meet my daughter. Modest hopes, but they kept a man alive."**

Former Alcatraz prisoner and escapee John Mason (Sean Connery) to FBI agent Stanley Goodspeed (Nicolas Cage). In this scene, Mason and Goodspeed are locked in separate cells in the abandoned prison by the renegade special ops team, and the anxious Goodspeed has been talking incessantly. Mason is referring to a "no-talking" policy initially established by the first warden of Alcatraz, James A. Johnston, in 1934; this policy was found to be unworkable and was abandoned in 1938. We find out in *The Rock* that Mason was incarcerated on Alcatraz in the 1960s, so although the screenwriters attempted to add a bit of Alcatraz history to the movie, they missed by almost thirty years.

BIBLIOGRAPHY

Babyak, Jolene. *Bird Man: The Many Faces of Robert Stroud.* Berkeley, California: Ariel Vamp Press, 1994.

Barson, Michael. *The Illustrated Who's Who of Hollywood Directors.* New York: Farrar, Straus and Giroux, 1995.

Buford, Kate. *Burt Lancaster, An American Life.* Cambridge, Massachusetts: Da Capo Press, 2000

Baxter, John. *The Gangster Film.* New York: A.S. Barnes & Co, 1970.

Clinch, Minty. *Burt Lancaster.* New York: Stein and Day Publishers, 1984.

Cohen, Mickey. *In My Own Words.* Englewood Cliffs, New Jersey: Prentice-Hall, Inc., 1975.

Eames, John Douglas. *The MGM Story.* New York: Crown Publishers Inc., 1982.

Esslinger, Michael. *Alcatraz: A Definitive History of the Penitentiary Years.* Carmel, California: Ocean View Publishing, 2003.

Finler, Joel W. *The Hollywood Story.* London, Great Britain: Wallflower Press, 2003.

Frank, Alan. *The Screen Greats: Clint Eastwood.* New York: The Hamlyn Publishing Group Limited, 1982.

Internet Movie Database, Inc. *http://www.imdb.com*

Karney, Robyn. *Burt Lancaster: A Singular Man.* North Pomfret, Vermont: Trafalgar Square Publishing, 1996.

Katz, Ephraim. *The Film Encyclopedia.* New York: Putnam Publishing Group, 1979.

King, Emily. *A Century of Movie Posters: From Silent to Art House.* London, England: Octopus Publishing Group, 2003.

Martini, John. *Alcatraz at War.* San Francisco, California, Golden Gate National Parks Conservancy, 2002.

McCabe, Bob. *Sean Connery: A Biography.* New York: Thunder's Mouth Press, 2000.

Nourmand, Tony and Graham Marsh. *Film Posters of the 70s.* New York: The Overlook Press, 1998.

Nourmand, Tony and Graham Marsh. *Film Posters of the 40s.* New York: The Overlook Press, 2002.

Odier, Pierre. *Alcatraz The Rock: A History of Alcataz: The Fort/The Prison.* Eagle Rock. California: L'Image Odier Publishing Co., 1982.

Parish, James Robert. *The Tough Guys.* New York: Arlington House Publishers, 1976.

Poole, Ed and Susan. *Learn About Movie Posters.* Chattanooga, Tennessee: iGuide Media Inc., 2002.

Reed, Walt. *The Illustrator in America 1860–2000.* New York: Harper Collins, 2001.

Sauter, Michael. *The Worst Movies of All Time, Or: What Were They Thinking?* New York: Carol Publishing Group, 1995.

Schickel, Richard. *Clint Eastwood, A Biography.* New York: Random House, 1996.

Sennett, Ted. *Warner Brothers Presents: The Most Exciting Years—from The Jazz Singer to White Heat.* Secaucas, New Jersey: Castle Books, 1971.

Tanitch, Robert. *Clint Eastwood.* London, England: Studio Vista, 1995.

Thomson, David. *The New Biographical Dictionary of Film.* New York: Alfred A. Knopf, 2003.

ALCATRAZ: The Movies

1937	*Alcatraz Island*, directed by William C. McGann

1937   *Alcatraz Island*, directed by William C. McGann

1937   *The Last Gangster*, directed by Edward Ludwig

1938   *King of Alcatraz*, directed by Robert Florey

1938   *Prison Train*, directed by Gordon Wiles

1940   *House Across the Bay*, directed by Archie Mayo

1940   *Passport to Alcatraz*, directed by Lewis D. Collins

1941   *San Francisco Docks*, directed by Arthur Lubin

1943   *Seven Miles from Alcatraz*, directed by Edward Dmytryk

1945   *Road to Alcatraz*, directed by Nick Grinde

1947   *Devil Ship*, directed by Lew Landers

1948   *Train to Alcatraz*, directed by Philip Ford

1950   *Experiment Alcatraz*, directed by Edward L. Cahn

1960   *Alcatraz Express* or *The Big Train*, TV, directed by John Peyser

1962   *Birdman of Alcatraz*, directed by John Frankenheimer

1967   *Point Blank*, directed by John Boorman

1968   *Skidoo*, directed by Otto Preminger

1975   *Alcatraz Breakout*, TV, directed by Jan Anders

1980   *Alcatraz: The Whole Shocking Story*, TV, directed by Paul Krasny

1984   *Electric Dreams*, directed by Steve Barron

1985   *Kicks*, directed by William Wiard

1986   *Terror on Alcatraz*, directed by Philip Marcus

1987   *Six Against the Rock*, TV, directed by Paul Wendkos

1987   *Force of Darkness*, directed by Alan Hauge

1988   *Slaughterhouse Rock*, directed by Dimitri Logothetis

1974   *The Enforcer*, directed by James Fargo

1979   *Escape from Alcatraz*, directed by Don Siegel

1993   *So I Married an Axe Murderer*, directed by Thomas Schlamme

1994   *Caged Heat 2: Stripped of Freedom*, directed by Cirio H. Santiago

1995   *Murder in the First*, directed by Marc Rocco

1996   *All Dogs Go to Heaven 2*, directed by Larry Leker and Paul Sabella

1996   *The Rock*, directed by Michael Bay

2002   *Half Past Dead*, directed by Don Michael Paul

ACKNOWLEDGMENTS

Foremost, I want to thank Vivian Young for her beautiful design and tremendous effort in helping to create this book; Susan Tasaki for her insightful and astute editing; Jolene Babyak for her remarkable expertise and in-depth understanding of life on Alcatraz; Sarah Lau for her skillful research and generous enthusiasm; Rich Weideman, John Martini, Nicki Phelps, Ricardo Perez, Craig Glassner, John Cantwell, and Katy Olds for sharing their Alcatraz knowledge; Clover Earl for graciously sticking through the book's many permutations; Alma O'Brien, Linda Chalmers, Robert Prado, Christopher Arpp, and Charles Odell for their ongoing support; and Greg Moore and everyone at the Golden Gate National Parks Conservancy for the incredible work they do, which inspires me every day. On a personal level, I want to thank my mother, Estelle Lieber, for instilling me with a strong work ethic (which kept me going these many months), and my father, Sidney Lieber, for raising me with an appreciation for film. Finally, I want to thank Howard Thornton for giving me the space (literally and figuratively) to complete this book and for his inexhaustible kindness, which continues to sustain me.

ABOUT THE AUTHOR

ROBERT LIEBER, an avid movie fan, trained as a graphic and product designer at the School of Visual Arts in New York City. After working for years in the art museum world—at New York's Guggenheim Museum and Whitney Museum of American Art, and the San Francisco Museum of Modern Art—Robert joined the Golden Gate National Parks Conservancy as a product developer; he has since introduced over one hundred and fifty park products, and written five children's books, *The Tallest Tree*, *A Lighthouse Saves the Day*, *The Flying Circus*, *Butterfly/Frog*, and *Catch Me* (the last two illustrated by Vivian Young), which were published by the Parks Conservancy.

FILMING ON ALCATRAZ: LOCATION MAP

● THE ROCK

1. Dock: Mercenaries, a renegade team of ex-Navy Seals, arrive on Alcatraz, pretending to be tourists.

2. "Chinatown"/west side of Building 64: Connery and Cage emerge from (nonexistent) tunnels; second missile is disarmed by Cage; Cage is taken hostage.

3. Below Post Exchange/Officers' Club: Final scene with Connery and Cage before Connery escapes from Alcatraz...again. Note: Cage is blown into the bay on west/Golden Gate Bridge side of island, but is rescued by Connery on the east side (boy, those tides are swift!).

4. Power House: Connery and Cage enter "tunnel" (this area is not open to the public).

5. Near Power House: Mercenaries drop bombs into "tunnels" in attempt to kill Cage and Connery.

6. North end of island: Site of missile explosions.

7. New Industries Building: Fight scene; Cage stuffs toxic nerve gas "green ball" into mercenary's mouth.

8. Plaza below New Industries Building: Cage waves flairs at a military jet and is blown into the water.

9. West Road: Cage runs from terrorists; fight scene.

10. Edge of Parade Ground: Cage and Connery argue about whether to leave, or to stay and try to disarm remainder of missiles.

11. Parade Ground below Lighthouse: Mercenary impaled on pole after being blown out of a window by an unarmed missile.

12. Lower Lighthouse: Missile and terrorist are shot out of (fake) lighthouse window (see #11); toxic nerve gas (in green balls) almost gets away from Cage (one is later used to kill a mercenary—see #7).

13. Cellhouse Roof: First missile—carrying nerve gas and aimed at Candlestick Park—is fired but diverted at the last minute by Harris, and falls into the ocean; Connery pushes a terrorist, who falls to Eagle Plaza near entrance to Administration wing.

14. Hospital: Terrorist command center, in which some elements are real and some are fake. Fake walls are shot up in the final show-down; site of Harris death scene, in physical therapy room; Connery takes cover in a bathtub, which is real (the tub was used by the "Birdman," Robert Stroud, while he was housed in one of the prison's hospital cells).

15. Recreation Yard: Connery is interrogated by Harris after his capture—Harris threatens a civilian with execution if Connery doesn't return the "seals" that activate the missile guidance system.

16. A Block: Connery and Cage are locked into cells, and escape. (Note: The method Connery uses to open the cells is pure Hollywood.)

17. Cellhouse/"Broadway": Mercenaries capture visitors and ranger to use as hostages.